For Mark, who left us too soon. You are sorely missed and will live on in the countless lives you've touched. Thank you for everything.

Cycletherapy: Grief and Healing on Two Wheels
Edited by Elly Blue & Anika Ledlow

This edition © Elly Blue Publishing, an imprint of Microcosm
Publishing, 2016
First printing.
Made in the USA

Microcosm Publishing
2752 N Williams Ave.
Portland, OR 97227
TakingTheLane.com
MicrocosmPublishing.com

Find more feminist bicycle books, zines, and art at
MicrocosmPublisishing.com

The *Journal of Bicycle Feminism* is supported by amazing
readers and select advertisers. To learn more, contact ads@
takingthelane.com

Cover art by Kenton Hoppas, who creates life-inspired
illustration, motion graphics, and video, found at kentonhoppas.
com

Get in touch with your submissions for the next book in the
Journal of Bicycle Feminism series: Money and Class. Please send
submissions and inquiries to elly@microcosmpublishing.com

CYCLETHERAPY

Grief and Healing on Two Wheels

Elly Blue & Anika Ledlow

Journal of Bicycle Feminism

Table of Contents

Introduction

Welcome to the first book in the *Journal of Bicycle Feminism* series. Expect a new book in the series every year or so.

Anika Ledlow, then an intern and now a colleague, came up with the topic a year ago. It was going to be a stand-alone zine, but submissions poured in.

By the time it became clear that the zine needed to evolve into something more substantial and less frequent, Anika had already compiled and edited an impressive collection of submissions reflecting a wide spectrum of feeling and events. I had collected other material that I wanted to publish about entirely different subjects, like carrying kids on a cargo bike or joining a women's cycling group in France.

I went back and forth deciding whether to keep the grief section separate or to try to integrate everything into a smooth read. I ended up going with the latter because the grief stories are all pretty heavy. And, fair warning, some of them are hella triggering.

But beyond that, as I shifted and rearranged the pieces of the puzzle, it seemed to me that they all fit together, that the tendrils of major life experiences reach into the more mundane or political ones, and that they are all rooted in every moment of our lives.

And in the end, most truly interesting writing is in some way marked by death or pain. Much of what people write about bicycling, specifically, is colored by a sense of vulnerability, of risk, of the sort of joy you rarely experience when the stakes are low.

In this age of social media, conversations seem to morph into polarized shouting matches about talking points. But there are always opportunities for slow, nuanced conversations about difficult topics, grappling with the personal in the contexts of bigger visions. Let this be another entry in that form. The stakes for society are, indeed, very high right now.

Whatever you do, keep pedaling,

Elly Blue

Portland, Oregon

December 10, 2014

Making Peace With the Wind

Barb Grover

Here's how Barb describes herself: "Birds, bikes, books, knitting, and travel preoccupy my thoughts. When not at work selling cargo bikes, I like to combine two or three from that list to see what fun I can have." She contributed to the second issue of *Taking the Lane* way back when, which has been out of print for years but is now available as an ebook again, which isn't as poetic a format as her writing deserves, but such is the price.

Today's east wind is unsettling.

Sailors tell tales of the horrors of the doldrums. In Samuel Taylor Coleridge's *The Rime of the Ancient Mariner*, windless water causes and represents an unsettling listlessness among seamen. We landlubbers know no such peril. For many of us it's the wind that is unwelcome. The wind bugs us: blowing dust, messing up our hair, pruning branches, slamming doors, and rattling windows, turning pleasant bike rides into ordeals. And, there's an unidentifiable aspect that just puts some of us on edge. It makes me pace and makes me pensive. Darn wind.

I've tried to make peace with the drafts that inhabit the world. One memorable attempt occurred on my bike, where first the wind shook me up and then turned me into a speck of dust.

I didn't start the day as a dust speck; I started the day as a bike tourist at the top of Coyote Mountain just east of San Diego. The wind farm near my campsite should have been a clue to the wind potential of this area. Indeed, I awoke to a strong west wind and knew I'd be buffeted around a bit at some point during the day. Wind in the morning is never a good sign.

As I crossed the mountains and began the descent towards the east, the wind not only continued, it also grew in force. The descent out of the mountains on Hwy 8 was at times treacherous. Forceful gusts pushed me around as I struggled to retain control of my bike, the wind's turbulent outburst shoving me off course, sometimes off of the shoulder and towards traffic.

As I neared the bottom of the hill, I stopped. The view into the Imperial Valley lay before me and it was not comforting. In the center of the valley a large sand storm raged. I consulted my map, estimated the path of the old road I'd planned to ride, and believed I'd be to the north of the storm.

No way was I going to turn around. There was only the tiny town of Ocotillo ahead. It proved not to have lodging or camping and I had no choice but to take my chances. As I took a quick north turn to hook up with the intended route, the wind hit me so hard it nearly knocked me over. I got off of the bike and walked the few hundred feet to my eastbound route. Picture my firm grasp on the bike, my bracing lean hard to the left, legs splayed, and barely staying on my feet as I shuffled along. After great effort I reached the intersection of County Highway S80 and turned to the east.

Now that evil crosswind was a tailwind. The earlier bout with the wind had left me a little shaken, and it took a few minutes to realize what was happening as I rolled into the center of the valley. The flat valley floor was passing by with amazing ease. As I relaxed, my speed just kept increasing. With little effort, barely even pedaling, I was cruising at 30 mph. It's really difficult for a cyclist to reach and maintain that speed on the flats, but here I was on a loaded touring bike just flying along. It was the dream tailwind of a lifetime.

I felt giddy from the speed. But visibility was decreasing, and I realized that I was heading directly into the sandstorm. I stopped, wrapped a bandana over my face, and carried on. The road was becoming harder and harder to see but I was still traveling at about 30 mph without pedaling. Awe at what was happening kept me in the moment. I felt no fear as I entered the center of the storm. Because I was traveling at the same speed as all of the sand and dust, I experienced no discomfort, my eyes were clear, my breathing unimpeded, my heart light.

Everything was happening in slow motion. Large pebbles, grains of sand, clouds of dust, all suspended and flying along next to me; all of us traveling by the same means and at the same speed. In that moment, I thought I understood the meaning of life: my life as a dust speck. With all of my intelligence, technology, and will, I was still at the mercy of nature, just like any other bit of sand or dust flying along with me. It was an incredible gift to truly know that. Thank you, wind.

The rest of that trip had some wonderfully pleasant scenic days and some trying moments on some awful highways, but for the most part it was the few miles on County Highway S80 that really defined the whole bike tour for me. Yet it didn't define my relationship with the wind. Back at home, the back door rattles and leaves fly across the yard, crows dive and turn riding the gusts, tree tops are bending.

The east wind is blowing and I feel unsettled.

Yes, Women Ride

Anna Brones

Anna Brones is the author of *The Culinary Cyclist*, which was the first ever book-sized book I had the honor of publishing. She has since moved up in the world and is anticipating the upcoming publication of her second book *Fika: The Art of the Swedish Coffee Break*, also illustrated by her *Culinary Cyclist* partner Johanna Kindvall and published, appropriately, by Ten Speed Press. Anna believes that bicycles really can change the world.

Eight AM on a Sunday is an early start no matter where in the world you are. In Paris it's practically insanity.

At this hour no one is out, except for a few stragglers still on their Saturday-night adventure and a few overzealous tourists trying to photograph the Eiffel Tower in the morning light. Otherwise it's just you and a few taxis, the city still groggy with sleep, quiet and empty.

On this particular too-early morning, I was biking across the Seine to meet up with a group of women at the regional express network (RER) stop at Jardin du Luxembourg. It was the inaugural ride of Paris Women Cycling Club. Maybe I didn't have to leave quite this early, but I was stressed about getting on the RER train with my bicycle, and this is something I did not want to miss.

Paris and I have had our moments. As much as I like a good city ride, more often than not I'm frustrated while on my bicycle here—any urban rider will know the feeling. Bus exhaust, a scooter zipping around you, a taxi driver who couldn't care less that you have the right of way.

But, this early on a Sunday, barely a soul on the road, the morning autumn light painting the buildings their glorious golden color—I couldn't be happier. Saint Germain, usually crawling with tourists, was empty and for once it felt like I had the city all to myself. The cobblestones, the churches, the buildings, the cafés—all the things that make Paris quaint to visitors but quickly disappear when you live there in the everyday mundane, they were all popping back out at me.

I downshifted and pedaled hard down Boulevard Saint Germain. With no cars, I could go fast. You see road cyclists pushing hard through the city on occasion. They whiz by you, and you wonder where they're headed; road cycling in Paris is only a means to get yourself out of the city. You look at their fancy frames and their uni-colored cycling kits and wonder if they're part of a team. For a few minutes that morning, I pretended to be one of them.

Postcard visions of Paris include fashionable women pedaling their town bikes in pencil skirts and heels; when it comes to the road riders, you're hard pressed to find any ladies. But in my almost two years in Paris, not once has one of these fast riders been a woman. They are always men.

I arrived at the RER station with plenty of time to spare and scanned the scene. A woman in a helmet and Spandex would be easy to spot at any time in Paris, but this early in the morning it was particularly easy, and I waved at the two women walking towards me, their bike shoes clicking on the pavement.

I had been invited to this ride by simple chance. I had been put in touch with the organizer, Silvi, for totally other reasons earlier that week. "Want to come ride with a group of women on Sunday?" she had written in her introductory email. How could I say no to that?

I am a cyclist, but more of an everyday cyclist than anything else. I believe in the bicycle as an everyday tool, something that can be used for sport, but that can also just be a means to everyday existence. For me the bicycle isn't an accessory, it's an essential part of life. I ride, be it to the market or out of town on the weekend, because it makes me happy. Because I love the feel of wind on my face. Because I like being responsible for my own transportation. Because I like the calming rhythm of pedaling. Because I like clipping in and going as hard as I can.

Pedaling on two wheels is such a part of my everyday life that I often forget that it isn't the norm, and that I'm lucky to be able to do it—particularly so because I am a woman.

What if I were told that I couldn't ride?

Certainly as women we are up against a lot in the Western world, and there's no denying the gender imbalance in the cycling world. But still—we can choose to ride. There are places where women aren't so lucky. Take Afghanistan for example, a country where a woman on a bicycle is very much breaking a taboo. The women in Afghanistan who do ride challenge gender norms every time they get on a bicycle. Not only that but they also risk their lives. Riding a bicycle isn't so far for some of the morality crimes for which women get imprisoned, or, worse, killed. But these women ride anyway, not to spark a revolution but because, just like me, they love it. They want to feel like they're flying.

I have been part of a team working on a film about these women. They come to mind often, especially when I am on a bicycle.

This summer was big for the women's cycling movement. On the last day of the Tour de France, a women's race was held immediately before the final stage. People had been petitioning for a long time for a women's version of the Tour, and while this single race was far from an entire three-week race. But it was worth celebrating, and I went out there and celebrated it.

With a press bracelet on my wrist, I got to stand front and center at Place de la Concorde, where the start line was set up. I was only a few feet from some of the best riders in the world. If I had tried to lock down a press pass for the men's Tour, it would have been a different story. But there I was, watching as the mayor of Paris, Ann Hidalgo, stood with the women at the start line, officially commencing the first-ever La Course.

A few laps on the Champs-Elysées compared to thousands of kilometers across Paris might seem like a small consolation prize, but, considering that La Course was held on the final day of the Tour de France, women's cycling shared one essential thing with men that day: worldwide press. Across the globe people watched women race bikes, proving that women's cycling is just as exciting as men's.

From where I was standing, I got to watch the women whip by twice on every lap. I didn't dare blink. The racers charged fearlessly over the cobblestones, the exact same ones that I ride over gingerly on rainy days for fear of an epic face plant in the middle of Parisian traffic. Hundreds of bicycles whirred loudly. Teammates of Marianne Vos stood next to me and cheered in Dutch. It was clear that I was in the midst of something historic.

Vos of course was the winner that day, her name in many headlines, but there's no denying that women's cycling had taken home the big honor. It was one step closer to being legitimized on a global scale.

But change takes time.

After a 45-minute RER ride into the southeast part of Île de France, a bit past Versailles, twelve women set out for a ride in Saint-Rémy-lès-Chevreuse. With rolling hills, a big protected natural park and a chateau every so often, this is a popular area for Parisian road cyclists. Every few minutes another group would ride past us. I hadn't seen so many cyclists in one place since earlier this summer on the Champs-Elysées.

We stopped so that one of our riders could fix a flat, the rest of us taking the opportunity for a water break. A group of men pedaled by. One looked at us, tilted his helmeted head, and said in a tone of complete and utter shock to his fellow rider, "bah, il y a que des filles!"

There are only girls! As if a group of women on road bikes were the strangest thing he had seen that day.

I shook my head and sighed.

France has a reputation for feminism, born out of the Revolution. In 1791 Olympe de Gouges published the Declaration of the Rights of Women, in response to the drafting of the Declaration of the Rights of Man. She was later guillotined. Simone de Beauvoir and French feminist theory have been taught in classrooms around the world. But, while France's historical reputation for feminism is strong, culturally things have stalled a bit. Women didn't have the right to vote until 1944, and France has yet to elect a female president. And, apparently, it's odd that we would want to ride road bikes.

That wasn't the only comment we heard that day. On yet another water break at the top of a hard hill, a group of older men rode by. "Bonjour les filles!" a few of them yelled. A nice friendly "hello," on a bike ride is always appreciated, but there was no denying the underlying subtext: these guys weren't used to seeing women on bikes.

Later on, two of the women got yelled at by a guy driving an SUV. He sped up to pass them and shouted "connasses" out the window, loosely translated: "bitches."

"I bet if we were men we wouldn't have gotten yelled at," said one of the women.

"Yeah, because then you would have had the right to be on the road," responded another.

I thought of these women riding in Afghanistan, women who often had rocks thrown at them when out for training rides. Certainly, France is no Afghanistan, but, in a country where women have all the same legal rights as men, why are we still being treated in this manner?

I asked one of my fellow riders if it was really that shocking to see a woman on a bike.

"Well, road riding isn't really that big of a deal for women," she responded, "but cycling overall is growing, and hopefully more women get involved."

We discussed the intimidation factor, the idea that if you're new to cycling, and a woman, it might seem overwhelming to go and get signed up at a mostly-male local cycling club. There is of course nothing wrong with riding in a mixed group of cyclists; in fact, the more the better, but there's no denying that there are some women who don't feel welcome in those groups, either because of fear or intimidation, and those women deserve an outlet to ride as well.

Just think of the "Ah! Women are riding!" comments you've most likely heard at one point or another; these words aren't the best motivator for you to jump in and ride in such a group, unless of course it's to power through and leave them in the dust. We are equals, we know how to ride, and yes, we deserve a place on the road or trail.

Which is why we have to band together—not just women, but everyone. Riding a bicycle is a glorious feeling, whether it's to commute to work or to win a race. We all have the right to enjoy that.

But for us in the U.S., France, or Afghanistan, on a road ride in the middle of the countryside or darting down urban streets, the bicycle remains one of the simplest and best machines we have. Shouldn't we all be encouraging each other to pedal a little more?

Pedaling uphill

Elly Blue

I wrote this essay in the middle of 2011 when every level of existence still felt immediate and precarious. Almost four years later, I'm pleased to report that life is a hell of a lot more stable, and the bamboo trailer is used more often to haul inanimate objects than it is to carry people who aren't feeling well.

I'm sweating and breathing hard, focused on the road directly ahead of my front wheel, pulling us uphill towards home. Joe is crouched on a sodden cushion in the trailer behind me, shivering under the tent of his coat. I'm in my rock-bottom gear, mashing down on the pedals, barely making it. It's 45 degrees and drizzling and I'm soaked with sweat under my raincoat.

There's a roar behind us and Joe says, "Watch out for the crazy person." Seconds later a late-model SUV zooms past us, far too close and fast on this narrow back street, and we both shout our indignation and alarm.

Thirty seconds later we pull up right next to the same car at a red light. We laugh and laugh. The light turns green and I stand up on the pedals to keep us moving forward. As I start to coast again someone smoking outside a bar yells "That's awesome!" and we wave back. For the first time in months, I feel fearless and free.

⇥

Joe has never been healthy, but he's been in nonstop motion in the two years we've been together, until the day, a few days into 2011, that he came to an abrupt halt. He was barely able to stagger out of bed that morning. He got right back in and stayed there all day, and the next day, and the next.

On his bad days in the past, we joked that we would build a "futon bike" so he could nap as I pedaled us both around town. It was a lighthearted fantasy. He'd always gotten better again after a day or two and I would put his health out of my mind. At 32 he seemed endlessly resilient.

But now days go by, and then weeks, and he doesn't get better. He continues his work from bed, barely skipping a beat. I have been struggling to launch my own business, but find it's just as easy to put on another pot of rice, draw a bath, or frown over medical websites as it is to sit down with my spreadsheets and strategic plans.

Just for a while, says my inner feminist, chafing at this gendered role. Then, more graciously: It's worth it. He would do the same for me.

One day we walk six blocks to a diner for breakfast. On the way back, he leans on me so heavily I nearly fall. When we make it home he collapses into bed and I start cooking lunch. That night neither of us sleeps as he tosses and turns from the pain in his knees and gut. I hold him and tell him he won't feel this way forever. I hope it's true.

One test finally comes back conclusive. It isn't one of the chronic diseases the doctor predicted, but something more terrifyingly vague: an invading army of yeast and bacteria. It took hold in earnest during a course of antibiotics almost a decade before and has slowly, painfully worked its way into all of his already troubled systems. He has been literally starving.

Armed with concrete answers and a heavy-duty prescription, Joe is energized, hopeful for the first time. Meanwhile, I crash hard. My muscles go sluggish and my mind becomes unwilling face the most basic tasks. For a month I've jumped out of bed each morning full of grit and glory, determined to get us both through the day and discover the way to good health. Now, with a clear path to follow, the exhaustion and fear hits me all at once. I plod through each day. At night, he's the one who comforts me.

I accept every opportunity to leave the house, but when I am away all I can think of is home. A friend takes me on a hike, another buys me coffee. I barter for a massage but by the time I get home from it all the tension has settled right back into my neck and shoulders. I halfheartedly pace through my days, cooking, working, curling up next to Joe to watch another movie, caught up in a malaise of my own.

Joe's doctor forgets to warn him that he will get worse before he gets better. It's a toss up, I think, which must be harder on him: the feeling of being kicked sharply in the guts all day, the monotony and helplessness of being trapped in his easy chair, or seeing my slouched shoulders and feeling he's a burden. Every night we discuss the events of our day, but there isn't much to share and what there is isn't much good. It is a low point.

Then we get the bike trailer and the world expands again.

We live in Portland, arguably the most bike-friendly city in America. Most of the people we know keep sizable fleets of two-wheeled machines in their basements and garages. I put the call out on Facebook for a loaner bike that can haul a passenger, and within an hour we have our pick of half a dozen options.

The first offer that includes delivery comes from a scrappy, self-taught engineer who is locally famous for the pedal-driven creations that come out of his garage workshop. He drops by the next day, his petite date pulling him and his bike on one of his trailers, big grins on both their faces.

The trailer is nearly as big as our bed and consists of uneven lengths of bamboo that appear to be barely held together with twine and shellac. He tells us it's stronger than steel and brags about how many times it's been run over and put back together. I can carry it up to our porch with one hand. They leave it with us to try out for the weekend, and we discuss it cautiously, hypothetically, neither of us willing to be the first to say that it is love at first sight.

That first night, we go out. Just around the neighborhood, less than a mile, back streets only. I'm sweating every intersection, taking the corners too tight and then too wide, terrified that someone in a truck will see me but miss my cargo. But I needn't worry—we're about as visible as it gets. We go to the library and then to a café to read and drink tea. Everyone is staring at us, but just being out of the house together feels cozy, almost normal. Then home again, where I help Joe up the steps before putting the bike and trailer away for the night.

We barely even need to discuss it—of course we'll buy the trailer. "Our first family car," Joe says proudly.

⇌

The next day I wake up feeling as low as usual, but agree to take Joe to his work for an hour and then bring him home.

The trip there is easy, but the way home is up a hill that has never seemed very steep before. Today, we're moving only a little faster than the dog walkers and stroller pushers on the sidewalk.

But I can feel the stress melting off as my heart pounds and my lungs heave and my legs go and go and go. I feel the knots in my back relinquishing their grip. Each pedal stroke engages the gears in my mind, jostling them unstuck, working them smoothly again around our life, the world, my own role and intentions. For the first time in long weeks we are laughing together, boldly fending off metal monsters, in collusion on two wheels each, the way we always have been at our best.

It's revelatory to see ourselves through the world's eyes. Nearly everyone has something to say at the sight of a small, red-faced blonde hauling a lanky man, half asleep in his pink sweatshirt. One day we find a heavy dresser on the side of the road and Joe perches on it as I haul them both up a hill. A child points, agape, and his dad takes out his cell phone to document the feat. It feels like winning a prize, as though the recognition were not just for the spectacle we make but for all of it, everything we're pulling through.

Then there are the men—always men—who shake their heads and ask, "Shouldn't that be the other way around?"

"No way," I gasp, if I have the breath. When we get home, I eat two meals in a row. I can't wait to go out again.

On the second day I suggest we go to the diner and Joe agrees, even though he's barely able to get out of his chair. As I struggle up the camber of the road in a busy intersection, a distracted driver swerves around us, just missing the trailer.

"I'm so sorry," I say, all the panic of our first ride, of his first weeks of illness, returning in a rush. "It's okay," he says. "I trust you."

The rest of the trip is level and calm. Maybe things will work out after all, I think.

⇆

As I become fitter than I've been in years, Joe gets better, slowly at first but then all at once. There are still bad days, but they're as rare as good days were a month before. My business plans start moving forward again. I meet friends and we laugh together. I'm still tending the house and exploring our limited culinary palette, but it's a choice, not an inescapable role. Sometimes I find an hour for the garden, where spring is just starting to wreak its sprawling green havoc.

One weekend afternoon a friend calls to ask if we want her old couch. I hitch up the trailer for the first time in two weeks and head across town. It's the kind of couch with a built in bed, and it weighs a ton. With the help of two neighbors, we struggle to carry it out to the curb. It clears the trailer's wheels by exactly an inch.

The ride home is nearly five miles and surprisingly smooth going. I take it slowly enough to engage with the questions of the men sitting on their front porches in the fading light. A mile from home I still feel good so I head five blocks out of my way, up a steeper hill than I would usually choose to take, to pick up Joe where he has been eating dinner at a friend's house. We ride home slowly, side by side.

By the time we get home my limbs are shaking and my stomach is a pit of emptiness. Our neighbors come over and lever the couch up the front steps and into our living room while I sit on the kitchen floor and eat bananas. When they leave, we curl up together on one end of it and fall asleep, equals in exhaustion and in victory.

Magazine

Sara Tretter

Sara Tretter lives, bikes, teaches, writes, and re-reads *Moby Dick* every few years, in Portland, Oregon. Her time travel story, "Henry's New Old Bike," should have appeared in the first *Bikes in Space* but didn't; you can hear her read it out loud in the audiobook version or read it yourself in the ebook and the second-print edition when that comes out.

The summer that I was 12, my next-youngest sister and I spent most of our days riding our bikes as far as we could. We lived in the suburbs of southern New Hampshire, but just outside the sprawl of our small city were forests, half-buried train tracks, and colonial cemeteries surrounded by crumbling stone walls, as well as tiny towns, the kind with a church and a general store around a grassy village center.

Emily and I didn't get along well. We are three years apart, which as kids made us close enough in age that we were on each other's nerves all the time but not close enough to be friends the way some sisters are. I was a tomboy, chubby, anxious, and bossy, while Emily was serious, glamorous even at 9 years old, and fiercely sensitive. Perhaps we took to riding bikes so much because we didn't have to converse, and it got us out of the house, away from our two younger sisters, who were 7 and 4 that summer. Probably my mom also encouraged it, as it got us out of her hair.

New Hampshire summers are hot and muggy, so we'd ride slowly, getting lost along the windy, narrow roads that cross back and forth over the Massachusetts border. One day we were completely disoriented and pulled over in front of a yard where an older lady sat in a plastic lawn chair, drinking lemonade. "Excuse me," I called out (for my mother had raised us all to be polite), "what town are we in?"

The lady looked at me for a minute with squinted eyes, as if she thought I might be joking, but I think she saw we were too young for a prank, and said, "Dunstable."

"Okay, thanks," I said. Then, after a pause, I asked, "But, um, excuse me, what state is that in?"

"Massachusetts," she said.

We made our way back to New Hampshire, though, when I think back on it I'm not sure how, as we didn't have any outdoor navigation skills, and this was long before cell phones. I think on those rides we just assumed that eventually we'd end up on roads we'd recognize, and eventually we always did.

One day we were riding not far from our house, along some fields between the road and our elementary school. If you were to ride this road today you'd be surrounded by subdivisions and gas stations and corner stores, but back then it was just open fields, not growing anything in particular, just tall grass and heather and cattails where the ground was marshy. Emily was riding in front of me, and she pulled off the road, hopped off her bike, and lay it down in the ditch where the ground sloped down away from the road and into the meadow.

I pulled my bike over too and stood over it. "What are you doing?" I asked.

She was walking toward something on the ground; I couldn't tell what. "I want to see what that is," she said.

We'd found some good things on our rides: animal skulls and shotgun shells, once a $5 bill. But as we got closer to the object on the ground, it looked like trash—an old magazine, its pages riffling in the hot breeze. Emily got to it several steps ahead of me, picked it up and cried out, "Ew!" She tossed it back on the ground.

I walked over and picked it up. It was a dirty magazine, filled with pictures of naked women. "Ew," I said too, but in fact I was fascinated. I couldn't stop looking at it, even though I knew Emily would make fun of me.

At 12 I was trying hard to figure out my body—and failing. I was clumsy and heavy and had pimples and braces and a spiral perm and was firmly in what adults call "that awkward phase." My mother and all of my sisters were slim and beautiful. I was a misshapen stranger in their midst. My younger sisters were too little to worry about their bodies yet, but my mom and my two older sisters, who were 17 and 18, had complained about theirs as long as I could remember. That this part was too fat, or too skinny, or too dark, or too curly. There was always something wrong.

To me their bodies seemed impossibly perfect. Long and slender and tanned and virtually hairless below the neck.

The women staring out at me from the torn and water-stained pages of the porno magazine were graphic and exotic indicators of what my body was supposed to be in the process of becoming.

My family was tight-lipped and awkward around the topic of sex. At nine years old I'd been given a book about how babies were made that centered on the premise of God helping a man and a woman find each other and fall in love and get married. So I had an understanding of the basics of sex, but had only ever seen drawings and my own parts—

which didn't look anything like what I was looking at in the magazine. I turned a few pages, enthralled.

I would think back to this moment the following summer, when I tried to use a tampon for the first time and totally failed. Sitting on the toilet, bathing suit puddled around my feet, legs spread wide, instruction page unfolded on the floor beside me, I cried and concluded that my body was just built wrong, I didn't have an opening there, and I flashed back on the women in the magazine, their vaginas gaping open, mocking me.

A few years later, finally acknowledging my crush on another girl, many moments in my life crystallized for me, and I thought back to the feeling I'd had with the magazine in my hands, fascinated, awkwardly aroused without knowing what it meant, just wanting to keep looking.

Many years later, in my early 30s, having carried my shame and hatred of my body into adulthood, I rejected a compliment from a lover about my body by pointing out some of its faults.

He asked, exasperated, "Who are you comparing yourself to?"

"Well, models and movie stars, obviously," I replied, in a tone meant to lighten the conversation, though of course it was true. And again in my mind I saw the women in the magazine, some of my earliest guides, outside of my family, for who to compare myself to.

"Sara, gross!" Emily yelled. I looked up. She was standing back over her bike, along the dusty edge of the road, waiting for me. My bike lay near her, on its side in the ditch. "Let's go!" she called.

I dropped the magazine back to the ground, and its pages lay still for a moment, the breeze having died down. The drone of cicadas in the meadow was dulled briefly as a car swept by, blowing Emily's hair around her helmet. I picked up my bike, trying not to look at her.

"All right, let's go," I said, and we pedaled down the road, our destination unknown.

Cycletherapy

MY BODY, MY CITY

Katherine Hodges

Katherine is from Iowa but has been living, biking, and photographing in Chicago since 1995. Google "Katherine of Chicago" to find her fairly active Flickr and Twitter and occasionally updated blog, *City of Destiny*.

I'd gotten my new bike in a hurry from friends after my beautiful vintage Schwinn cruiser became too costly to fix. But my new bike's handlebars went haywire one day as I tried to bike to the Blackhawks championship parade. I had a couple shops tighten them but they always came loose again. I brought it to a friendly and popular neighborhood bar about a mile and half away. That bar was becoming my main hangout because of a budding friendship/flirtation with a bartender. He was always asking me to leave my bike in the bar, and one night I stayed after closing while he fixed it. It held longer than any fix I'd had from an actual bike shop.

On my birthday in late August, I had drinks at another local bar with friends, then more joined me at my main one. I drank excessively and, uncharacteristically, danced. My friends left and I should have gone home, maybe in a cab. The bartender had helped me with one the previous week when I sat outside in a depressed mood. But instead, I biked to the 4 AM bar we'd gone to two weeks earlier. My mood shifted from joy to a depression I have sometimes, feeling apathetic and unable to keep myself safe.

I only wanted to talk to the bartender I knew, but he was too busy. I talked to a man I probably wouldn't have otherwise. I accepted his offer of a ride home, though I lived six blocks away. In the car he had cocaine, a drug I don't do. He came up to my apartment and stayed for two hours. There were drugs and beer and humiliating things that I went along with, and he took photos of me on his phone. I couldn't stop him. He hadn't been violent or hurt me physically. I didn't go to the hospital or police. But I know I didn't want any of it to happen.

In the morning, confused, I had the first hangover of my life. By evening I felt well enough to retrieve my bike. I didn't drink all weekend. I wrote a couple friends online about my strange birthday night and saw the friends who'd given me the bike and told them a little.

I started to realize it wasn't a bad hookup; it was assault. I'd been too drunk to consent. I told the therapist I'd been seeing for two years. Then at my second bar one night, a week after the assault, I revealed it on Twitter. After I went to the sketchiest 4 AM bar in the area, met a man, and went home with him. I didn't mention the assault. It went well, but I knew this wasn't healthy.

I needed to tell the bartender, but it's hard to talk at someone's busy workplace. And even though I got to tell him a few things about that night, we didn't get to the whole story.

Bicycling felt good and got me out of the house. The assault happened in my office/living room/bedroom, where I spent nearly all my time, and I didn't want to be there. But sadly the routine and repetitive motion of cycling went along with the obsessive thoughts I had hundreds of times a day; "You stupid whore. You dumb drunk slut. You're trash." No one had said these things to me and I didn't believe them, but they were there, no matter how well therapy went or how much I read about rape culture. I'd replay the night and think of the "NO!" I'd been unable to say. I knew it wasn't my fault. I knew it wasn't my punishment for all the drinking and the guys I'd been with earlier in the year, but I couldn't stop the thoughts.

One day as I stood on the street, a car full of young men slowed and threw an egg that hit the wall behind me. By the time I got on my bike, enraged, I was too late to chase them down. But I found a piece of concrete and rode miles looking for an excuse to be goaded into throwing it to defend myself.

I biked in unsafe mental states. One night, despairing I had no chance to talk to the bartender, I biked to a northern suburban demolition site I'd been photographing and tried to sleep in the field across from it. I'm not sure why. Punishment? It was cold and I couldn't sleep. I panicked when it hit the exact time the assault happened weeks earlier. Finally, I got up and treated myself to a coffeeshop breakfast on the way home.

I took a week off drinking to clear my head. Then I drank at a house party and had pot, which I'd expected there, and coke, which I hadn't. I did it to erase the circumstances in which I'd last had it. I left and biked to the bar in a downpour, drunk and high on two drugs, and just sat there because it felt safe.

I visited a lot of bars that October, partly to explore Chicago and partly to prove one bad guy couldn't stop me from having fun. But some nights got out of hand. Multiple bars, aimless angry biking, and more guys I'd just met, including the first visitor to my apartment since the assault.

Then the first friend I'd told, my closest friend the past few years, started to question my story. He thought, since I'd been drinking and violence wasn't involved, I had "complicity;" it couldn't be assault. It's hard to capture the despair I felt. At least I finally told the bartender, via a handwritten letter. The next time I saw him, he immediately hugged me. He believed me. The month ended with finally telling two friends the whole story in person, the first to hear it besides my therapist.

I didn't drink all November to save time and money, but also because I knew, though I'm mostly responsible and rarely drank at home, the nights I'd overdo it were scaring me. I had so much grief over my lost friendship that actively self-destructive urges resurfaced. I didn't trust myself to even get home safely on the 10-minute ride from the bar. So I substituted alcohol with coffee shops and diners and drinking pop at the bar.

I had great times there without alcohol—and even stood up to drunk guys harassing me about being "shy" or "nervous." I suddenly lost the second friend I'd first told about the assault and was glad I could resist drinking myself into oblivion. My moods stabilized and I had fewer obsessive thoughts. I told the bartender I'd soon be back to normal drinking there. He said, "You don't have to booze it up. I just like getting to see you smile."

Time, therapy, and acquaintances and friends who stepped up to support me when other friends rejected me terribly, are healing me. I've resumed more responsible drinking and biking. The bartender seems dismayed I ride in Chicago's tough winter, but even though biking can be more dangerous, I feel safer in the cold. I go home as fast as possible. I don't want to keep the night going by sitting outside the hot dog stand or peeling off snow-soaked clothes in front of a stranger. I want to stop using bicycling for an endless escape from my feelings and start using it as a way to feel comfortable in my body and my city.

Cycletherapy

Bicycle Epiphanies

Karen Canady

Karen Canady asked if I would the prefer the lyrically descriptive version of her biography or the self-promotional one. I urged her to lean on in. Thus, she tells us that she is a mild-mannered patent attorney who moonlights as an apparel manufacturer. She created Bikie Girl Bloomers, a line of versatile, comfortable clothing, to help women integrate bicycling into their everyday lives. You can learn about her patent services at canadylortz.com, shop her clothing at bikiegirl.com, follow her tweets @bikiegirl1, view her photos on Instagram via #showusyourbloomers, and like her Facebook page at Facebook.com/BikieGirlBloomers.

Meditation takes many forms. Some people sit still and quiet, seeking to clear the mind of all thoughts. Not me. I can achieve a meditative state only while at least some part of me is moving. The action must be one that does not require concentration or close attention, one that resides in muscle memory. Knitting works, but only if it involves a mindless pattern, like garter stitch or a simple rib. My preferred mode of moving meditation is bicycling.

January 2004: I decided to get out my beloved bike and go for a ride along the beach. The voice of Dido, singing "My Lover's Gone," kept playing in my head as I rode. It was incredible to feel my body moving, the breeze flowing over me, after four weeks of spending most of each waking hour in a hospital at his bedside. The line played over and over in my head: "My lover's gone, no earthly ships will ever bring him home again." I stared at a ship just far enough out in the ocean that I could not quite make it out. I knew I had to make peace with the loss, and find a way to accept it without making sense of it. I knew I could not make sense of his death any more than I could get a clearer view of that distant ship, no matter how long I strained to focus on it.

Pedal stroke by pedal stroke, I felt it all: my hurt, my strength, my breath, my loss, my heartbeat, my love, my tears. The truth behind all that I felt was that I was alive, very much alive. The richness of these feelings reflected the richness of my life. How lucky to have been touched by this experience. I took a chance on love again. The brevity of the marriage did not diminish the beauty of finding love and sharing myself with someone else again. There was nothing to regret. There were memories to savor. Yes, there were also tears, but I let them roll down my cheeks to celebrate the proof that I was alive and fully human.

On the way back towards home, a flat tire disrupted my pedaling meditation. When I realized it was more than a punctured inner tube—my tire had busted open—I had to call my ex and the kids to come rescue me. The wait gave me time to consider whether to get a new tire for my dear 15-year-old Nashbar or let go of my beloved quirky parallelogram-framed bike I'd proudly purchased as a grad student. I knew I had to get back on the bike again soon, so postponing my decision to repair or replace was not an option. There were new shifting systems that work better than using the old levers on the down tube, and manufacturers had started making bicycles that better fit the dimensions of a woman's body. I decided that a new bicycle could be my metaphor for moving forward and embracing the new.

The new bike meant I was riding more, both commuting by bike more often and getting out for longer rides whenever

I had a kid-free opportunity. Grief dominated that first year of widowhood, but the bike rides were my peace and comfort. No matter how shaky I felt inside, the ocean was always there, holding steady for me. Feeling the power of my thighs reminded me of my strength.

It was during these rides I reconnected with my internal compass. I did a lot of beach rides that year. The mindlessness of following a path without intersections allowed me to let my mind wander in reverie. I had ridden that beach path with Bill several times, struggling to coast enough to slow down and match his meandering pace on that cheap hybrid bike of his. It hadn't been easy to let go of my usual habit of keeping my cadence up, enjoying a little speed, snickering to myself as male riders picked up their pace after the ego-bruise of being passed by a woman. With Bill, I learned to ride for the scenery, to notice the houses along the beach, to relax about the pace, and to experience my surroundings more fully.

But Bill was gone, and I was riding on my own. I had to ponder this, and ponder it a lot. The truth of his death, and the permanence of his death, had to be repeated in my mind a thousand or so times for that truth to sink in. After all, death sucks. You can be a good widow day in and day out, taking care of the kids, keeping up with what must be done at work, holding yourself together, paying the bills, and staying in touch with friends. You can keep this up for days, weeks, even months at a stretch, but after all that dutiful coping, he's still dead. Good behavior does not bring him back. The big triumph is simply getting up again the next day and putting one foot in front of the other. And doing that again and again, the same way my feet, clipped in to the pedals, keep circling back around. It's the same repetitive motion, but somehow it is getting me somewhere.

Cycletherapy

STROKE

Joe Biel

Joe Biel is a writer, designer, filmmaker, teacher, activist, and founder of MicrocosmPublishing.com and co-founder of the Portland Zine Symposium. He is the author of *Beyond the Music*, the director of the film *Aftermass: Bicycling in a Post-Critical Mass Portland*, and he tours with the Dinner and Bikes program. He has been featured in *Time* Magazine, *Publisher's Weekly, Utne Reader, Oregonian, Broken Pencil, and Maximum Rocknroll*. You can read more of his story in his memoir, *Good Trouble* coming in February 2016.

In 1983 my dad had his first stroke. I mostly remember this day because my babysitter stayed very late, no one told me to go to bed even once the sky had gone pitch black, and no one would answer my questions.

My mom finally came home from the hospital and I was told the basics: My dad had suffered a stroke at the steel mill that day. He had casually tried to pass it off, and his co-workers had just as casually decided he might as well leave the line and go to the hospital.

Six years later, my family had still never talked about it. Well, unless you count my mom's frequent violent outbursts. She blamed my dad for every one of our family's problems and failures, and for each time my sister or I acted out. She blamed him for his inability to parent, let alone control his muscles well enough to walk or talk. She screamed at him for his "selfishness" while bludgeoning him with her fists.

As a child, I accepted my mom's version of events. I had few other viewpoints to even consider. But it still didn't seem right to blame my dad for the thing that had taken away almost all choices he had in life beyond what channel to watch on TV. I could tell that it was hard on him, too.

As I grew up, I knew in the back of my mind the violence my mom inflicted on our whole family could result in our being taken away from her. But that's the problem of dysfunction—the predictability of it is comforting in a distressing way. If I called Child Protective Services, my sister and I would be put in a youth home where, I suspected, the abuse might be even worse.

So instead I stayed away from home as much as possible. I rode my bike to the comic book store after school every day. I went so frequently that I knew the schedule of every employee. There were things that I liked more than comics. But this daily visit did what I needed it to. It allowed me to slowly build bonds with people I was not related to, like other people who were into comics, played nerdy board games, and eventually people who made their own comics and zines. These bonds helped me trace a path back to morality in the years before I discovered punk rock and its cousin, xerocracy.

By the time I was a teenager I found myself able to trust and invest in people, and even began building relationships. My situation was widely known in my neighborhood and was plain to anyone who saw my family together for an hour or two. There was no shortage of sympathy, but I just found that awkward. Peculiarly, most people framed my mom as the victim of the situation, an analysis I was now old enough to be dubious of. I remembered that the violence had started before my dad's stroke. Even so, it was nice to be taken in by other families and see what healthy relationships looked like. I almost never went home, and most people in my neighborhood understood without ever quite naming why.

I turned eighteen, survived two gruesome car accidents, began my life as a dedicated bicycle commuter, and moved out of town. It was a path to freedom from my past.

I didn't fully realize how much the situation had affected my perceptions until my dad's funeral in 2007. Seeing the array of photos artfully hung in the funeral home, I learned for the first time that my dad had been in the military, stationed in Alaska after World War II. I remembered that he had been funny. My only living memory of him, before what we referred to as "his accident," was riding with him in his tiny hatchback. He taught me how to hum along to *The Pink Panther* song on the radio. Even though he was 49 when I was born, he knew how to relate to me as a child. He couldn't be a part of my life for most of the time that our lives overlapped, but he had known exactly how to make me feel wanted and involved in what was going on in a fundamentally vital way.

Thinking about things that way at his funeral, surrounded by my friends who had come even though we'd grown apart a decade before, I learned the most fundamental lesson that my dad taught me: Despite all hardship and treatment by those around us, we still have each other.

GUAYAKÍ
·BRAND·
YERBA
MATE
COME TO LIFE

FIVE SPOKES OF GRIEF

Julie Brooks

After corresponding for years, Julie Brooks and I finally met at a conference in Pittsburgh recently and I am happy to report that she had the biggest smile of anyone there. She describes herself as a writer, rider, bicycling activist, and roving researcher of the wholly remarkable galaxy of Western New York. She also wrote the feminist zine reviews at the end of this volume and is currently working on co-creating a zine for women over 40 who ride bikes. She can be reached at rocbikewriter@gmail.com

⇆

"There are dreams of love, life, and adventure in all of us. But we are also sadly filled with reasons why we shouldn't try. These reasons seem to protect us, but in truth they imprison us. They hold life at a distance. Life will be over sooner than we think. If we have bikes to ride and people to love, now is the time."

-*Elizabeth Kübler-Ross*

⇆

In her 1969 book, *On Death and Dying,* Elizabeth Kübler-Ross puts forth a stage-based, non-linear model that attempts to explain people's life-threatening or life-altering experiences with terminal illness, be it their own or of someone close to them. In more recent years her "five stages of grief" model has been applied to divorce, significant break-ups, substance, physical and sexual abuse, and other encounters with trauma, and it continues to represent a dynamic and flexible framework for uncovering and clarifying the ebb and flow of emotional shock.

When I was a student at The University of Wisconsin, I rode my bicycle to campus every day. In the mornings, as the fog was lifting above Lakes Wingra and Monona, and streetlights were dimming with the rising sun, I'd mount my metal steed and pedal a four-mile trek to campus, weaving through the Vilas neighborhood, skirting Camp Randall Stadium, pumping up North Charter Street and Observatory Drive, and finally bouncing down the cobblestone roadway to Memorial Union for my morning cup o' Joe. These rides provided me with opportunities to joyfully bask in the simple moments that passed before my mind became saturated with the theoretical perspectives framing my study of Abnormal Psychology. In the evenings, while the golden sunset sunk behind the lakes, these rides offered transition time, palliating whatever struggles I may have experienced during the day so that I could be present for whatever might be waiting for me at home.

On one unforgettable April morning, I was rolling along in my usual exuberant manner, comfortably pedaling the streets I'd been traveling for several months. The weather was chilly, but I felt cozy and relaxed in my lobster claw gloves and scull cap. My helmet was secure, my lights were blinking, and my pack was snug against my back. I wasn't in a hurry. And, I was feeling good about the day ahead.

I don't know anything about my assailant, what they were thinking, or what kind of day they were anticipating. I don't know if they were sober or drunk, oblivious or seething with anger about the cyclist delaying their commute to work. I don't even know if the driver was a man or woman, traveling alone or carting young children to school. In fact, I would never know anything about the hit-and-run motorist whose passenger-side mirror clipped my left grip, forcing me sideways into a parked car and over my handlebars.

DENIAL

I was fortunate. When I hit the ground I was conscious and relatively pain-free. My bike had fallen behind me, away from passing traffic. And I was quickly able to get both of us onto the sidewalk before a pedestrian stopped to see if I was okay. In the immediate moments following this mishap I felt physically fine, and my bicycle seemed to be intact. So, after graciously thanking the passerby, I proceeded on my way. In the coming days, however, handlebar-shaped bruises began to form across my quads, and my right shoulder and arm throbbed incessantly. Still, I expressed little concern about what had happened, pooh-poohing my friends' worry when I started riding my bike again. "I have to get back up on the horse sometime," I'd tell them. Then off I'd go.

ANGER

Three months later, my outward show of denial was quickly appropriated by the death of a bicycling buddy, Brian. When I learned of this hit-and-run, something inside of me snapped. I couldn't sleep, I was eating little, and I was riding my bicycle more aggressively, putting myself in dangerous situations late at night—and on roadways I had no business traveling. "I'm not going to let some hit-and-run goon determine how safe I feel on the streets!" I'd declare. My bike was no longer my deliverer of joy, but rather an instrument I was using to antagonize others, and perhaps, punish myself.

Eventually the bruises on my legs healed and the pain in my shoulder and arm began to dissipate. Internally, however, I was a wreck. For months after Brian's death I became enraged whenever I heard about a bicyclist being intimidated, struck, or killed by an automobile driver. Those earlier feelings of joy relished atop two wheels were now eclipsed by my urgent need to retaliate. I became a belligerent crusader, self-righteously separating myself from others and looking for opportunities to light into people about bicyclist's rights on the public roadways.

DEPRESSION

It took me years, and the help of others, to reign in my rage toward negligent or seemingly clueless motorists. Though I was no longer seeking revenge or pugnaciously confronting unapologetic car drivers, I continued to exhibit and express little patience for people who didn't understand the virtues of bicycling. Oftentimes I would just melt into a debilitating despair when family, friends, and unknown others would wonder, "Why do you have to ride in the streets?" or glibly state, "The roads are for cars."

BARGAINING

Eventually I started riding my bike more cautiously and responsibly, and I became a bicycling activist. My anger, rage, and depression had served important purposes. Ultimately, I reasoned, compassionately connecting with and educating others—riders, drivers, and foot-travelers alike—would be more beneficial to alleviating some of the stress we all faced on the public roadways than remaining imprisoned by my smug and alienating attitude.

ACCEPTANCE

Today, I continue to commute by bike. I love pedaling the streets around town: the feel of the saddle I've cured over time and the bulge in my leg muscles when pumping up long, steep hills. I'm keenly aware of my vulnerability and mortality, and I celebrate my ability to feel across the spectrum between exuberance for the adventures I continue to enjoy alongside others and the rage and despair that occurs when I hear of another cyclist being hurt or killed. Life will be over sooner than I think, and I have no idea how that will occur. In any event, I do have a bike and am surrounded by people to love. Now is the time.

Cycletherapy

ARIEL

Gretchin Lair

Gretchin Lair still misses her bicycle Ariel, stolen just days after what was to be their first and last trip to the beach. "My quaint Ariel... Our revels now are ended." (from Shakespeare's *The Tempest*)

Cycletherapy

The Other Deepest Thing

Erin Fox

When the topic for this volume was announced, I kept expecting—maybe dreading is a better word—an influx of overtly religious submissions. When zero came in, though, I was a little disappointed to be missing that perspective. So I was thrilled when Erin Fox slipped us this beautiful piece right under the wire. She tells us that she grew up in a small town and now lives in Portland, Oregon. She likes God, flowers, light, wide-open spaces, and her bicycle.

I check out some books about grief from the library. I feel stupid because grief seems like a noble feeling reserved for those who have just come home from a funeral. I know it's more complicated than that, though. I know when my Papa was in the hospital to have surgery on his heart, even though he lived through it, I had all sorts of grief because I realized that even if it wasn't time yet, he was eventually going to die. I was totally overwhelmed by the simple physicality of a loss like that . . . how my Papa took up a six-by-three-by-one rectangle of space in the universe and how one day he would not. I think when he does die, the whole planet will heave with despair about that change, about the new and awful emptiness of the space that for so long was taken up by his molecules and cells and papery skin and aftershave.

⊐

When we broke up, I felt the same way I did about my Papa: "Therefore my spirit fails, my heart is numb within me." Psalm 143, a lamentation, a poem about grief, disconnection.

I got sick and I was afraid to leave my room, but I didn't cry for months.

"In the morning let me know Your love," the Psalm also says. But with grief, time is different, and the morning behaves strangely—after a year the sky turns a lighter blue, but then a bad dream or a tough day and it's back to the darkness for a while longer.

⇋

On my nightstand is a book of poems, written by a friend of a friend, about how his father died. I'm embarrassed to tell this friend of a friend how much of a real friend he has become to me in those poems. How they are the only things big enough to hold my grief right now, how they are the first bit of morning that I see. I don't even know him, but, after months of not being able to cry, I weep over his grief and my grief and those poems. I know they are about dying, about fathers dying, but I swear that I do understand them. I think, when you love someone and you are watching them leave you, it doesn't matter as much if they are driving away fast in a car or disappearing slowly in a hospital bed. What matters is that awful emptiness that's left behind.

⇋

When we were together, I dreamt that we were riding our bikes along a highway lined by wheat fields. We were naked and the sun was setting and there were no cars anywhere. We were riding slow and fast at the same time, and I felt free and whole and greatly loved. I feel this way a lot when I ride my bike, so I know it was not you who made me free or whole or loved. You were in the dream because you were the person that I wanted to share feeling that way with.

⇋

Cycletherapy

Real love is a hard and holy endeavor—it is not a way to fill the holes in your heart or to distract you from learning to love your worst self. A real breakup is not the loss of your spackle or false mirror, it is the loss of the person you picked to share your free-est, whole-est, most loved self with. That is a real loss, and I feel it now in my chest like a ball of lead, pinning me down to my bed when I try to get up in the morning.

How do I talk about this weight? My hands shake just thinking about it. Depression is such a scary word to me; I hate it. I think of a man I saw once through his living room window, just sitting in his chair, unable to move and staring at a blank television screen. I think of the Buddhist story of a woman who carried her daughter's rotting corpse with her everywhere, her mind lost to grief. Is this me now? Is this me forever?

Half the pain of being sad is worrying about being sad, hating yourself for being sad, being filled with the despair that you will always be sad. Depression makes you feel uninteresting and inconvenient and unlovable. I meditate a lot, watch my thoughts, say over and over, "This is not you, this is a feeling, this is a thought, this is not you." I am sobbing in my best friend's car when I notice in myself a horrible certainty that she hates me for crying like this. I squeeze her hand to remind myself of what is real and, in defiance of depression's dark inventions, I sob harder. Why does it happen like this, my mind trying to cut me off from the things I need most right now?

When it gets really bad, the very best thing I can do for myself is to move. I move slowly. I take walks where the only goal is to walk. In my room I dance, making slow and sweeping movements, my body mourning for me in ways my heart still cannot. I trust my body now much more than my mind. My body says, You can always keep breathing. You can always keep moving. You are still alive, connected to the air and the ground and the light. In my chest and throat and the space between my eyes, I feel a sensation of being permanently welled up. I know I need to cry more, that the weeping I do over the poems and with my friend from time to time is not enough.

It is hard because a part of me still believes that I do not deserve to be this sad, that tears, like books about grief, are for those suffering "real loss." But tears are just water, I tell myself. Like water from the shower, water from the rain, water from a river or an ocean; like the water you lived in for eight months before it broke down your mother's strong and shaking legs. You cried for years after that, I tell myself. You were grieving the loss of living in another's body, the loss of being so close you shared a heartbeat. You didn't worry about the appropriateness of your tears, of your sadness. You just wept and ate and slept. I cross everything off my to-do list. "Weep," I write. "Eat," I write. "Sleep."

I let my garden go, and it becomes strangely abundant— with weeds mostly, but also with new flowers, and raspberries. *Eat* is a thing on my to-do list, so I pick the berries and nothing else. I start to dress in ways that comfort me; I think of myself as a swaddled baby and wear three sweaters at once. I take a homeopathic remedy that is supposed to help me cry. Weirdly it does, though maybe this is because each night, after I put it on my tongue, I say, "I love you"—once to my sadness, once to my fear, and twice to myself.

⇘

"Perfect love casts out all fear." This is from somewhere in the Gospels, books we grew up with and loved together, but did not always believe in. This is a thing that we both believed, though, a thing we lived out with each other and with our friends. It is something I believe in now more than ever, something I am watching happen over and over again in myself.

After more than a year of learning to give my love and acceptance to fear, to sadness, to me, I feel less pinned down. Each day is its own, and some are better than others, but mostly things feel lighter now. I have come to terms with the fact that I am lonely. So many of my friends have moved to far-off places, but you are farther away than any of them. I am trying to be okay with all of it, though. I open my heart to the love that's still around, even if it's coming from unexpected sources. I take slow, quiet walks in the evenings. Each time I do, some part of the earth breaks my heart open—the warm wind, the full moon, the largeness of a tree—and I am flooded with the relief of being loved, of being seen and held. The earth is lonely too, I think, with so many people being too busy to look up and really see it. The earth has a lot of grief, has seen a lot of grief. I am doing my best to make it a friend. I often wish you were here with me on these walks, but sometimes that expansive ache of aloneness feels so very free, and I am surprised at how much I like where I am right now.

⇆

I had a teacher once who grew up in a small village in southern Mexico. His Abuelita used to tell the story of a bull that would roam the streets of the village at night. If you heard the bull coming, it was with a click-clack trot that grew faster and faster the closer it got. Once you heard the bull, there was no way out; it would find you and it would hit you. If you ran from the bull, you might be able to keep ahead of it for a while, but it would always catch up, and when it did it would hit you and explode into a giant pile of shit that would cover you and your home and your family and everyone around you. If, however, you heard the bull and you turned to face it, it would still hit you just as hard, but it would explode instead into a million pieces of gold.

The only thing I know about healing is that you have to turn and face the bull of your grief. There is a poem I like that says, "If you want to know kindness as the deepest thing inside,/ you must know sorrow as the other deepest thing." And that's the gold you get for facing and passing through your grief, for fighting to know love and peace in the midst of isolation and despair: kindness. Kindness towards yourself, towards the suffering of the earth, the suffering of the sick and sad and worried and dying. Kindness that heals and strengthens and transfigures and redeems. Kindness that changes things and reveals things and ever so slowly *makes things better*.

⸺

Tonight I am riding my bike, and as the light fades and everything gets watered down and quiet, I go ahead and face the bull again. It's a kind of giving up, giving over, letting go. It's a kind of dying. My friend does some hospice work, and she says that a good death is one in which the person dying feels ready. Those people die with their eyes soft and dreaming, letting the blow of the bull's horns wash over them in slow motion. She says you can almost feel it as their pain subsides, as they begin to see the gold.

Enter into your sadness like this, I tell myself. Die the death you've been given, die all the thousands of deaths you'll be given in this life. Die with your eyes soft and dreaming, ready for what comes next. In the midst of the grief, feel the gold.

It is sunset and I am riding down a highway with no cars, whole and lonely and free, going slow and fast at the same time. The light overwhelms my eyes, and I am filled with the sense that this is an ending and also a beginning, that the sun is setting and rising too, that this is some kind of morning because I feel in my bones the love I've been so desperately in need of. I know it in the trees and the wind and the feeling of peace that comes from acceptance, from life being enough. "For ye shall go out with joy, and be led forth with peace: the mountains and the hills shall break forth before you into singing, and all the trees of the field shall clap their hands." This is from the book of the prophet Isaiah, not a lamentation but an invitation, a promise. The earth radiates it, every person I've ever loved calls it out to me from afar. It is kindness, it is the blood pumping in my legs and in my heart. It is some deep and knowing part of myself shouting, You are brave, you are loved, you are loving! The lead ball in my chest still hurts, but it's real and it's glowing and it's burning up smaller and smaller every time I breathe in, breathe out. It makes me strong and it makes me alive. Another night would not shine like this; another heart would not break like this. This grief is all my own.

Cycletherapy

Riding the White Line

Connie Oehring

Connie Oehring lives in Colorado and works as an editor for a small book publisher. Her essays, reviews, and poetry have appeared in several magazines, and she is the author of *Meeting the Bear and Other Poems* (PS Press, 1996), a letterpress chapbook. A longer version of this essay first appeared in *The Missouri Review* 18, 2 (1995).

There are images sharply fixed in my memory from my youngest sister's disappearance in 1980. One is the face of her murderer, who in the weeks before her death stopped his car twice to offer me a ride as I walked the mile and a half home from the bus stop. Another is a confused vision of this man dragging Doris off her bicycle and into his car. Nobody saw this happen, but it comes to me when I try to understand her death, to comprehend an essentially senseless act of violence.

Sometimes I remember my sister's blue bicycle lying in the ditch, with her backpack still strapped to its carrier. I never saw this either, but nine years after her death I collected the bicycle from the coroner's office and brought it to my older sister's house. She still has it, at the back of a storage shed, though I doubt anyone will ever use it again.

I call these pictures memories because they are the way I remember what happened, and they have shaped my life in ways that her murderer, now dead, could never have imagined.

⇆

My father bought two Huffy Olympia 10-speeds when I was fifteen, bringing home one for me, one for my sister Jill. He said they were rewards for our straight A's that year in high school, but I think we probably would have gotten them anyway. Both bikes were orange, so we distinguished them by wrapping the handlebars in different-colored tape. I had one yellow bar, one red. Jill's were black.

My father showed us how to assemble the bicycles. He had purchased them at Woolworth's in Fairbanks and brought them home, in pieces, in large boxes. We installed seats, handlebars, pedals, and wheels. We adjusted brakes and derailleurs. We couldn't wait to ride.

We lived in a rural residential area outside Fairbanks, and bicycles were our only way to get around. The public transportation system—borough buses that were few and far between—was still new, uncertain, and expensive. We lived thirteen miles from Fairbanks, eight from North Pole (where we attended high school), and miles from most of our friends. We were in the habit of bicycling long distances, and we knew how much easier the 10-speeds would make it. It was a kind of new freedom: going farther faster and with less effort.

Bicycling was not something we thought of as exercise; it was strictly locomotion, and there was always a goal at the end of the ride. Sometimes we chose to ride to school rather than take the bus, or to bicycle into Fairbanks and back to see a movie or eat a banana split at Dairy Queen. Once, when I was about twelve, my mother and all five of us children rode slowly into Fairbanks for dental appointments, a trip that took most of the day because Doris, then six, crawled along on her little bike. There was always somewhere to go or something to do within reach—though not always easy reach—of two wheels.

When I was sixteen, two of my sisters and I bicycled to Denali National Park, 150 miles from our home. My bicycle, which had developed chronic hub and axle problems, came apart near Ester, about 30 miles into the journey. We called our father and waited until he arrived with fresh axles, grease, and wheel bearings. On that trip I replaced my rear axle three times and Jill's once, not to mention at least one flat tire. The first night we slept on a pole line just off the highway before Nenana, about 40 miles from Fairbanks. The next morning we stopped for water at the fire station in Nenana and spent some time talking with a young firefighter named Reggie. He marveled at our trip—this was in the days before bicycling had become so popular that you expected the shoulder on your way into the mountains to be lined with pedalers in Lycra clothing. But he also had a patronizing air, as if he didn't expect us to make it.

It didn't help when we discovered that the ride to Nenana had been the easiest portion of the journey. After that, we climbed steadily into the mountains. We often had to get off and push our heavy bicycles to the tops of the steep slopes. By the middle of the second day, our leg muscles were quivering with exhaustion, and we stopped to rest during the heat of the afternoon. When Reggie checked on us later that day, we had just started riding again. He was amused that we were only about twenty miles from Nenana. We were sunburned and tired and took his joking in bad part.

When we rolled into Denali on the morning of the fourth day, we felt vindicated and triumphant. The rear wheel of my bicycle was in bad shape again, and we were clean out of axles, so we decided to take the train home. But first, we took our little day packs, tied the tent and sleeping bags to the bottoms and tops of them, and spent three days hiking around the Denali backcountry. In the tent campground near the park entrance, we met travelers from all over the world, hitchhikers and backpackers who sat around the campfire and talked and sang with us. We were travelers too.

⇆

A couple of years ago I bought a new bicycle, replacing the old Huffy I'd had for fifteen years. It had been years since I bicycled regularly, or at all, though I kept the old bike with me, moving it into new sheds, basements, and yards everywhere I lived.

When I moved from Fairbanks, Alaska, to Boulder, Colorado, I rode it a few times, but never with pleasure. I told myself it was too old, needed too much work and money to put it into reasonable shape. Daylight walks and hikes were okay—actually, anything in company was okay—but when I was alone, a feeling of imminent danger accompanied me everywhere. On at least one occasion, walking home after dark from a friend's house two blocks from mine, every pair of approaching headlights sent me into a panicked crouch behind the nearest hedge or tree until the car had passed.

⇆

I spoke two times to a man who would have killed me if the circumstances had varied by a hair—if he had met me a little later or a little earlier, if I had been smaller (like my sister), or a shade less alert.

Before I faced my fear—which took years—bicycling was an easy thing to give up. After all, it had always been frightening on one level; I did know the literal danger of exposure on a flimsy, unstable pair of wheels to the fast-moving automobile traffic in which cyclists must mix. However, that risk was manageable; I could always persuade myself that I was too smart, too careful, and too quick to be in much danger. This second level—the more visceral exposure I felt, raked by all of those passing eyes and not knowing what kind of notice they might be taking—was different. My sister's killer cruised the highways and saw her as an easy target. Whenever I throw my leg over my bicycle, I know that I could become that kind of target for anyone at any moment as long as I'm on the road.

↜

My attitude toward bicycling started to change when I was a senior in high school, even before my sister's death. Unlike most of my friends, I didn't have access to a family car. I still took pride in the fact that I got around on two wheels, and my friends expressed awe at my feats of mileage. But I also started to worry about my weight and took to riding the nine miles to school daily, swimming a mile before school, staying after school for swim-team practice, then bicycling home. I limited my food intake to carrots and apples. I had a friend and partner in this behavior, whose particular obsession was running. She used to have another friend drive her fifteen miles up the highway so she could run home. We compared notes and kept food and exercise logs. We both became very thin and felt dizzy walking upstairs. This pattern lasted most of the year, and my memory of any other activities at the time is hazy.

↜

During the second part of the school year and through the summer afterward, I had an afternoon job at McDonald's and frequently cycled the thirteen miles each way. On rainy days I took the borough bus, but I liked bicycling when I could because it was keeping my weight down. Yet, even though my feelings about bicycling and its place in my life were changing in ways that were intimately connected to my feelings about my body and myself, I always felt safe on a bicycle. Sure, there were always those near misses on the highway, but I still felt in control, able to wheel my way anywhere in perfect freedom.

⇋

That summer, when I was eighteen, Doris was kidnapped and killed by a passing stranger. She was riding her bicycle home from a swimming lesson in North Pole, late in the afternoon, in broad daylight along busy residential Badger Road. That day I worked from three to eight PM and arrived home sometime after ten, having as usual spent an extra hour in the crew room. I rode home in the bright late twilight of the Alaskan summer. My mother burst out when I entered the room—"Where have you been?!"—and then, when she had calmed somewhat, told me that my sister wasn't home yet. But her bicycle had been found. My brother and I spent hours trying to think of possible solutions to this mystery: Doris had gone to visit a friend, had run away, had had an accident. But we couldn't explain away the discovery of the bicycle with her backpack still strapped to the carrier, a clear indication that something much worse had happened. When my father arrived home later after helping to search the brushy woods all around the place where the bicycle was found, he would only say, brusquely, that he was certain she was dead. In fact she was, though we were not to learn it for certain until her murderer confessed three years later. (A few hours afterward, he killed himself.)

Badger Road was honeycombed with mazes of developments, trailer parks, and networks of gravel roads like ours, but it also had long lonely stretches. It's a twelve-mile loop of paved road that starts from the Richardson Highway six miles southeast of Fairbanks and rejoins the same highway at North Pole. We all knew every inch of this road, which had a friendly shoulder for bicycling. We had ridden it hundreds of times in both directions. Drivers who honked and waved at us were frequently people we knew. When we took the borough bus, we walked the mile and a half from Badger Road to our house, set back in the typically dense birch and spruce forest of the Tanana Valley.

Now no one knew where my sister, eleven years old and just entering seventh grade, had gone. Suddenly people who had praised us for bicycling everywhere were critical of my parents for allowing us to go so far alone and unprotected. A manager at McDonald's, an older woman, told me she didn't know how my mother could forgive herself.

Doris disappeared on June 13. For the rest of that summer, I continued to ride my bike to work and to visit friends as I always had. My parents never tried to stop me. My sisters and brother didn't stop bicycling either, as far as I can recall. One slight rearrangement was that when I worked late, my mother drove in to pick up me and the bicycle after my shift. I had a strong feeling that it was important not to be afraid, even though on some level I hoped to see that man, who would indeed turn out to be the murderer, again. My brother had seen him talking to our sister the day before she was taken, and I had recognized the description of him and his car, although it would be years before I mentioned my own encounters with him to the police. I did mention them to my father when they had happened, who went from near catatonic to enraged in less than a second and shouted at me to never take rides from strangers. That was enough to dissuade me from speaking more of it then.

I did make one major change in my route on the way to Fairbanks. Instead of riding along Badger Road all the way to the Richardson Highway—a busy road, but largely uninhabited between Fairbanks and North Pole—I slipped in by the back gate of Fort Wainwright and rode through the post. This way I felt I was closer to telephones and large numbers of people, and that was true. But I was also exposed to whistles, comments, and propositions from passing soldiers. These small harassments, which I might earlier have taken as compliments, filled me with rage. One day a soldier followed me slowly for blocks, holding the door to his truck open and urging me to climb in. I finally stopped and screamed "Go away!" so fiercely that he slammed the door and roared off.

At the end of summer, I moved to Massachusetts for my freshman year of college. I dismantled my Huffy, which now had several thousand miles on it, and took it with me. When I unpacked, I reassembled the bicycle, stood it in a corner of my dormitory room, and never really used it again.

⇆

At first it was not easy, but I have taken to the shoulders of the roads again, sometimes with my husband but usually by myself. There are things I had forgotten about bicycling— the trance of slow motion, the way the countryside wraps itself around me, the hum of wind in my ears. The air has a sweet, dusty smell and rings with the voices of insects and birds. Grasshoppers spring away from my tires as I ride, or try to hop the other way and rattle through my spokes. I fall into a dreamlike state and sometimes find myself singing softly.

On the highways, the white line is my magical safety guide; as long as I can keep on the right side of it, I feel secure. Around here, too many of the roads have no shoulder, and I have to ride the wrong side of the line. I sometimes find myself trying to balance along it like a tightrope walker. When a car gets too close, I automatically swerve away and sometimes leap right off the pavement. So far I haven't had any tumbles, but when I do, I hope I'll fall the right way—away from the road. And I'm fully aware that any feeling of security is relative. I'm not in that safe automobile bubble that we're all so accustomed to—there is nothing between me and any kind of harm but air.

Things still shake me when I'm bicycling. A shout from a car window, even if I don't understand the words, will make me start planning escapes in case the driver decides to stop. I'm alert on lonely side roads. Once, while bicycling on a long straight stretch, I watched a man walking ahead of me suddenly disappear into a tall stand of corn. I was riding uphill, moving more and more slowly on the long grade. I had a sudden attack of fear: perhaps he was waiting there for me and meant to leap out and grab me as I passed. I didn't have the speed to sprint away from him. So I moved to the other side of the road and watched for the place where he had vanished. When I reached it I saw that the corn hid a long, narrow driveway, and the man was walking up it with his back to me, already a hundred yards away. I felt foolish and couldn't help wondering how long it would be until I could walk or ride without fear.

Every day I hear or read stories of women attacked in public places where it would never occur to them to feel unsafe. Even on a bicycle, you have no advantage over someone who suddenly springs out and knocks you over. Or someone else on a bike who can move faster than you. Or someone in a car. Fear can stop you from taking that chance. Slim though the risk may be, it is a terrible one, and many women end up leading locked and cautious lives, hemmed in by the possibility of violence.

But I have gradually reached a balance between my fears and the pleasures that go side by side with them. Today, I can't help thinking of bicycling as exercise. But whenever I climb on the bike and start rolling, it means more because it evokes those old feelings of freedom that most teenagers get—perhaps—with their first car. I got mine with a bicycle, then lost it for too many years. The countryside around here, with its wide-open spaces and the contrast between the mountains and plains, helps keep that feeling spinning along with my wheels. My new bicycle is a 21-speed hybrid, a road bike with straight handlebars, a comfortable seat, and wide, 27-inch tires with an inverse tread. It's not built for speed, but it's meant for exactly the kind of thing I do—highway riding. It also takes kindly to the gravel and dirt roads that wend their way among the farms.

Many of these details still feel new to me, though I have lived here for years now and hiked often in the mountains. There are things I don't notice from the car—wildflowers growing in profusion along the shoulder, for instance, or a particular combination of a lovely old gray barn, an ancient farmhouse, and an enormous stack of hay bales far enough from the road that I never would have glimpsed it at fifty-five miles per hour.

⇆

My old Huffy was nearly unsalvageable. Its tires had rotted, and the wheels were rusty. The derailleur and brake cables were also rusted and stiff. The seat cover had sprung several holes, and the foam stuffing was gouged and rotting.

I managed to get the tires to hold a little air and rode it once slowly around the block, then left it in the yard. Shortly afterward, it disappeared. I suspect that my husband put it out in the alley for the garbage collectors, though he claims to have no recollection of such an act. I suppose the builder who finally cleared his junk pile out of our yard may have loaded it up by mistake, though he denied it too. I don't know if I could have gotten rid of the Huffy on my own, so I guess it's just as well.

Meanwhile, even traffic doesn't quite prevent my bicycle dreaming. It feels almost the way it used to, when I composed poems in my head on the way home from school or work, then wrote them down as soon as I reached home and paper. I'm having to recompose now—ideas like "safe" and "free" will never again be unqualified for me. But they're words that mean more with every mile.

❦ **INTERVIEW** ❧

Cycletherapy

A Different Road:
An Interview with Delicia Jernigan

Anika Ledlow

Anika Ledlow is our former publishing intern and the editor of the Grief & Healing section of this volume. She says of herself that she enjoys iced tea, freshly picked radishes, and helping people out. I'll embarrass her by adding that she is also friendly and curious and makes stunning visual art as well as writing sharp academic studies about gender and violence. She can be contacted at aledlow@reed.edu.

About a year ago I had the pleasure and privilege of interviewing Delicia Jernigan, the founder of the So Many Roads Tour, a friend of my mother's, and the person who inspired the theme of this publication. I had just arrived home from my own summer bicycling trip when my mother told me about Dee. After losing her brother Anthony to suicide, Dee cycled from Portland, Oregon to Portland, Maine to re-center herself, tell her brother's story, and raise awareness about suicide. My life, like many others, has been touched and changed by depression and suicide. Dee's story inspired and amazed me. I knew that I had to talk with her and am so very honored to share her story.

Tell me about your tour.

It was my pilgrimage. It was releasing feelings about my brother's death that I didn't even know I had. And I wasn't just riding for my brother. I made a memorial wall on Facebook for everyone and put whatever message they wanted on it. I wasn't searching these people out; they just came to me. Thousands of people saw what I was doing.

What were your goals for your ride?

My goal changed throughout the ride. I started out with the intention of raising awareness. But it was also about sharing my brother's story and encouraging people to do whatever it was they wanna do. After Anthony died, I realized that I wanted to take advantage of my time—I wanted to inspire people to live their lives.

What were you feeling on your bicycle?

I think I was just so vulnerable. Vulnerable, of course, to traffic, but also I was just a person out there telling a story about a person close to me. It was very emotional. My heart was broken, and then I was physically kicking my own ass and talking about this tough subject. But thank goodness I was vulnerable. That's when you grow the most. You don't know where you're gonna eat, where you're gonna sleep. You can receive. You're authentic. It takes you out of what you've been doing your entire life. You know you're doing what you set out to do.

What surprised you the most on your trip?

The number of people I ran into who'd lost people to suicide. Everyday I'd meet somebody. And that's what I wanted to do—to reach out to people.

Tell me about a person you touched with your bike trip.

In Idaho Falls I was meeting some mothers who had all lost children to suicide. It had been a horrible day—wind, heat, four flats. I get in there, riding through construction, and there were people cheering for me! They were those three mothers! They gave me huge hugs and I got to eat dinner with them. They all shared their stories and I even got pictures. I think it helped them to show them the point of view their children were going through.

What was the worst part about your trip?

I didn't have any bad experiences on that trip. The worst of it was the 20 flats I got from Portland to Minneapolis. This country—and world—is filled with wonderful people who want to help. I stayed with so many types of families. We warn each other about what's out there, but I just told myself that there are good people. Whatever you put out you will get back, you just need to give everyone a chance.

What's one thing you would change about your ride?

I spent an entire summer carrying the baggage I didn't need. We think, "Oh man, what if this happens?" Don't worry. You have everything you need and you'll be able to collect it along the way. I know what I need now, I know what I don't need.

If you had the chance, what would you say to yourself on the first day of your tour?

Keep pedaling. There were days I didn't wanna bike anymore. But you have to keep pedaling. If my brother had come to me, I would have begged him to keep trying. That's why I called it the So Many Roads tour. It was important to me to do something of huge importance to demonstrate to people that this person was so incredible. I had to take the advice I would have given my brother, to keep pedaling. Who knows what tomorrow has in store?

Is there anything else you want to tell me about your tour?

Yeah, I wanna to tell you a story: I had just crossed into super hot and muggy Minnesota and I had no idea what was in store for me. I had never been there before and the road I had planned on taking was closed, so I had to take another route. Not only did a 72-mile day become an 84-mile day, but all the traffic was coming around on the back road, whizzing past me on a road with no shoulder and all I could think was "Please don't hit me."

About 60 miles into it I got away from everyone. I was riding along and I saw a lake in the distance, the first one! I could feel the rain in the air and then it started to sprinkle. I got to the lake—and it was so beautiful. Minnesota was the only state I had seen that hadn't been affected by the drought.

I started crying. I just lost it. I thought, "Man, I really changed the game." I started talking to my brother and really thanked him. Losing him was such a hard price to pay to get this motivation. I felt so grateful and so proud of myself.

Then I had to laugh at myself a little bit. People were riding by, asking me if I was okay, and here I was sobbing on the side of the road in front of a lake.

Maybe I needed to get that tired to get everything I was feeling about it. It's been three and a half years but I think it will always be like this. I try to be present. I have never been so present as I was on that bike trip. You have to be present when you don't know where the hell you are.

We have so many choices to make in our lives. I took a different road when the tragedy happened.

↪

You can read more of Dee's story on her blog: somanyroadstour.tumblr.com

Cycletherapy

᪥ **FICTION** ᪥

The Crash

Lauren Hage

When not writing, Lauren Hage can be found shipping packages at Microcosm Publishing, playing with her cats, or reading at the park. She wrote an essay about running away from home by bike for the Childhood issue of *Taking the Lane*. You can find more of her writing and art at laurenhage.com.

"Are you okay?" asked the passerby, reaching his hand out to the young woman laying on the pavement.

"What happened?" asked the young woman. She looked up at the man and noticed the graying hairs starting to encroach on the sides of his hairline.

"What's your name, Miss?" he asked, brushing the broken glass and street dirt off her shoulder.

"My name?...why am I here? How...," she said looking around at the small crowd that had formed.

"I think you may have a concussion. Here; sit over here on the curb. The ambulance is on its way now, I hear it down the street."

"What happened?" she asked.

"You got hit by a truck. You were on your bike, all that's left is the bent frame. I'm amazed you are alive," the grey haired man said. "Here have my jacket," he added. "I don't want you to go into shock."

"Your jacket, it smells familiar, the cologne..." said the woman.

The ambulance made its way through the jammed street. The paramedics jumped out and starting looking her over.

"Do you have an ID, Miss?" asked the paramedic. She searched her pockets and came up with nothing.

The truck driver was standing across the street talking on his cell phone and gesticulating. He glanced her way but didn't come over.

"Ma'am, what's your name?" asked the fresh-faced paramedic, then glancing over at the older man as he shook his head from side to side while shrugging his shoulders. "You appear to have a mild concussion. We need to take you in and make sure that you don't have any internal bleeding or broken bones."

"My bike! What happened?" said the young woman as she was lifted into the back of the ambulance.

She woke up again in a hospital room.

"Hey, there you are, how are you feeling?" said the older man.

"Hi, much better, except I still don't know my name or where I live...do we know each other?"

"Ha, when you say it like that, it sounds so fated. I came back to see how you were and to get my jacket back," he said smiling and picking up his coat from the blue plastic bag with the rest of her clothes in it.

A nurse breezed in with a lunch tray. The man sat down on the window ledge, pulling his shirt tail down in the front so his pot belly wouldn't show.

"Well, what name do you want to be called?"

Cycletherapy

The young woman stared up at the ceiling and squished the green Jell-O in her mouth as she contemplated, "How 'bout something with an M, like Marcy."

"That sounds nice... I had a daughter named Melanie." The man stared down at his worn leather shoes.

"Had?" said the newly-named Marcy, still a little giddy from the painkillers.

"Yeah, she was only 6 when she died, at this very hospital in fact...cancer."

"That's terrible, it must have been so hard... By the way, you never told me your name." said Marcy, trying to change the subject, as she sat up on the side of the bed to face him.

"Bernard, Bernard Sheller."

Marcy's eyes lit up as she looked over at the plaque on the hallway wall, "Are you *that* Bernard Sheller?"

"Yep." He said humbly. "After Melanie died, I donated her college fund to this hospital to help others like her. All I wanted to do after that was focus on my work and my business did well, so I kept giving the hospital my profits. Eventually, they named a wing after me."

Marcy took a deep breath of the dry hospital air. "Well Bernard, the nurse said I can leave if I have someone I know accompany me. You seem like a safe bet, since they know you and all?" She brushed her long dark blonde hair into a ponytail as she spoke.

"Are you sure?" said Bernard.

"If not you, then who else? I can't just wait around for someone to find me and tell me who I am, but how do we even start?..." she said grabbing the bag of dirty, blood-stained clothes and headed toward the bathroom to change.

"Here, don't put those dirty things on. Let me get you something from the gift shop," Bernard said sliding off the window sill and heading out the room. "You just take a shower and I'll be back in twenty minutes with some clothes for you."

Marcy stared with amazement at her newly-formed friend; all she could muster was a "thank you."

Bernard knocked on the bathroom door, "I have your clothes here. I'm not looking," he said holding out the bag with his head turned toward the window.

Marcy cracked open the door and reached out for them.

"I found a way we might be able to find out who you are. The boy at the gift shop said that he is a bike commuter too. He suggested tracing the bike to the shop where you bought it and checking to see if they have your name on file with the serial number. Luckily, I grabbed what's left of your bike. I was planning to use it for a metal art project... that's mainly what I do now," he said gazing out the foggy window to the street below.

"Well, I'm glad you haven't melted it down just yet. I'm ready," said Marcy. She came out of the bathroom wearing a pink sweatshirt with a pattern of hearts and rainbows on it and matching bottoms.

"I'm sorry. That's all they had that came close to your size, everything else was for infants," he said with a chuckle.

"It's okay, they're actually quite comfortable, thank you."

Marcy followed Bernard down the long hallway, trying hard not to peek into the small recovery rooms. Bernard signed her discharge papers and they continued out to the parking lot.

Bernard unlocked his car trunk and pulled out the wreckage, "Here we go, it's a bit of a mess but the serial number is clear. I don't see any kind of bike-shop marking or sticker, though..."

Marcy started to feel overwhelmed, "What if I don't like who I was?"

Bernard finished writing the string of numbers down in his pocket notebook and flipped the cover shut, "There's only one way to find out." He shut the trunk lid and gave her a smile, "I say we start with the closest bike shops and work our way out. Sound good to you?"

Marcy nodded her head and got into the passenger-side seat, "Do you think we could get something to eat first?"

"Of course, how about burritos?" said Bernard, "I know just the place."

Cruising down the boulevard made Marcy feel even more disoriented. The scene of the truck that had hit her flashed before her eyes; she quickly rolled down the window, stuck her head out, and vomited.

Bernard pulled over and shut the car off. "Is my driving that bad?" Bernard said in a half-laugh.

"No, it's not that. I...," Marcy got sick again, "...I had a flashback of my accident."

"Well, lucky for you the first shop is just at the other side of the block. Maybe we'll luck out," said Bernard, offering her a handkerchief.

Marcy smiled and took a sip from the public drinking fountain, "Normally, I'd never drink out of those things. Hey! That's a good sign right? I remembered something."

They walked into the shop and quickly realized they only sold used bikes.

"I don't think they'll be much help here," shrugged Bernard.

"You never know." Marcy said with her new-found optimism. "Excuse me, do you have a record of your sales with serial numbers?"

"Bike get stolen?" asked the lone, purple-haired mechanic.

"Sure, you could say that," Marcy shot Bernard a smile.

"Let's see, got the number?" asked the mechanic, fumbling through a grease-covered binder, blowing the hairs out of her eyes.

"Here it is," said Bernard, flipping to the page.

"Nope. Sorry, we don't have a record of ever selling a bike with that number."

Bernard looked up at a sign above the counter that read: "Rent a bike, only $10 a day."

"You know the next bike shop isn't that far. Are you okay to ride?" asked Bernard.

Looking up at the sign, Marcy replied, "That sounds like a great idea!"

They picked out their rides and headed to the next shop.

The wind in her face made her feel at home, safe. Then another flashback came to her, but this time it wasn't of the accident but of her former life, sitting at a desk in front of a computer, in a room full of cubicles. She was taken aback at the mundane work atmosphere, "I think I was a telemarketer or something?"

"Another flashback?" asked Bernard.

"Yeah."

"That's really good to hear, let's hope more comes to you," he said trailing behind, a little wobbly on his cruiser-style bike.

"I forgot how fun this is," he said weaving in and out of the bike lane.

"Be careful!" shouted Marcy. She was trying to keep up her spirits. She didn't want to be a telemarketer.

They chained the bikes together and went in the next shop. This one looked more promising, with newer models on the showroom walls.

"I'll ask this time. You stay here and catch your breath," Bernard said. He was huffing and a little sweaty. Marcy stayed outside in the afternoon sunshine, barely breaking a sweat from their short journey.

"No luck here. How about that burrito?" Bernard said blocking the sunlight with his body.

"Sounds good."

"Don't give up just yet, we have plenty more to go...is anything looking familiar around here? Your crash happened just a couple of blocks that way."

Marcy shook her head no, and they got back on the bikes.

"The food cart is just around this bend here," Bernard pointed at the quaint curved alleyway lined with rose bushes.

"How do you know about this place?" Marcy asked.

"I use to work at the bank across the street, years ago."

They got off the bikes and walked the rest of the way, through the aisle of food carts and people.

"This is it. They have the best burritos in town," he said leaning his bike on the picnic table Marcy had picked out. "Do you know what you'd like to eat?"

Marcy shook her head. "I'm up for anything."

With the smell of the fryer grease filling the air, Marcy froze in her steps; the sight of a restaurant, with a large blue cup as the logo, gleamed in her head.

"Here we are. Dig in," said Bernard, sliding Marcy an oversized burrito wrapped in parchment paper.

"Thanks. Do you know of a restaurant with a blue cup as the sign?"

Bernard had already bitten into his steaming hot burrito. "Another memory, eh?" he said around the food. "Yes, I do indeed, that's the Mug Café on the other side of town."

"Can we go there next? I swear this is the last rabbit hole. If we don't find out something concrete, I give up."

"Well, let's keep up hope, but it's your decision." Bernard reached out and gently placed his hand over Marcy's.

They finished their food and hopped back on the bikes. Night was approaching and they pedaled fast to return the bikes, worried about making it to the café before it closed. Right across the street from the bike rental shop was the commuter train.

"We can take the train across town, it's faster than driving, and the stop for the café is just a block's walk," said Bernard, a little wheezy from the ride.

"Great!" said Marcy pumped from the adrenaline rush, "If I didn't love biking before, I do now. That was intense!"

Bernard smiled as they boarded the train.

"Thank you so much for helping me out like this. I'm practically a stranger and you've been like family," said Marcy as the sun set.

"It feels good to be needed. I've missed that feeling." Bernard said breaking their gaze as he stared down at his folded hands in his lap.

Marcy returned the act of kindness, reaching over and grabbing his hand to hold.

Just then, the familiar cologne scent Bernard was wearing flashed her back into childhood. She was sitting underneath a Christmas tree and lying beside her was her father. He had worn the same cologne.

"You got that look in your eyes. Did you remember something else?" Bernard said laying his other hand on top of hers.

"I remembered my father. He went out for a last-minute loaf of bread for Christmas dinner. He never came home. He told me, 'Jessica, I'll be right back. Love you.' That was the last time I saw him."

"Jessica—that's a nice name." Bernard said, smiling with sad eyes.

"I don't feel like a Jessica. Please, call me Marcy."

"As you wish."

"Don't you need to call your wife? You've been out a while, won't she be worried?"

"Actually, a couple years back we separated. She remarried and has a new family. I go and visit sometimes."

Marcy didn't know what to say, so she just nodded her head and looked out the windows at the blur of strangers on the street.

They arrived at their stop and hurried down the block. Turning the corner, Marcy nearly bumped into a woman around her age.

"Oh, I'm sorry, excuse us," said Marcy.

"Jessica! I've been looking all over for you! Your face, that bruise, what happened?" said the woman glancing between the two, with her short, black, kinky hair bouncing in the evening breeze.

"She got hit by a truck this morning and has slight amnesia," Bernard said, clearing his throat.

"What do you mean? Jessica, who is this man? Say something."

"This is Bernard. He's been the sweetest, trying to help me find out who I am," said Marcy.

"You remember me now, don't you? Let me give you a hint," she held up her left hand and showed Marcy her wedding ring, "You don't wear one because you're afraid that when you're working someone will rob the bank and take it..." Her face fell. "They called today, Jess. You've been fired. Too many skipped days. I'm sorry."

Marcy started to tear up, as a flood of emotion came over her.

"Erika... I'm so sorry," said Marcy as she held out her arms, "I don't want that stupid job anymore."

Marcy let out a sigh of relief. She knew who she was again. She felt more whole than ever.

"We didn't know what to call her, so she picked out Marcy," said Bernard, hands in pocket.

"Marcy. I like it," said Erika, giving her a kiss on the cheek.

"I remember everything now," said Marcy, "but I'm only going to keep the parts I like. That includes both of you."

"Come have dinner with us. We live just up the street, above the café," said Erika to Bernard.

"Yes, you have to. You can stay in our guest room. It's late and your car's so far away. How do I ever repay you?" Marcy said.

"You've repaid me by making me feel like my old self again, so thank you for that, and I do think I'll take you up on that offer. I sure am tired," said Bernard, dabbing the sweat from his brow with his handkerchief. "Since you're out of a job, do you want to come work with me? I could use the help at the metal shop."

"That would be grand," said Marcy, as the three of them walked up the street home.

Cycletherapy

❧ JOURNAL ❧

Cycletherapy

The Xtracycle Diaries

Jamie Passaro

Jamie Passaro lives, writes, and bikes in Eugene, Oregon, where she is experiencing empty-bike syndrome now that her younger daughter rides her own bike. Passaro's essays, interviews, and articles have been published in *The Sun, Utne Magazine, Oregon Humanities Magazine, Oregon Quarterly, Forest Magazine, Culinate.com, NWBookLovers.org* and *fullgrownpeople.com*, among other places. Reach her at jpassaro@q.com.

Last fall, my daughters and I set out to ride our bikes to and from their schools—about a three-mile round trip—as frequently as possible. My seven-year-old, Olive, usually rode her mountain bike and my four-year-old, Vivienne, rode on the back of our family's Xtracycle. We commuted through hail and sleet and tantrums. We took the family cat to school one day in the Xtracycle's panniers. Here are excerpts from the journal I kept of the year.

SEPTEMBER 25, 2013

Ollie and I are riding home from school; she's on the back of the Xtracycle. It's cloudy with occasional spits of rain, the tires slapping wet pavement, Ollie chattery as she sometimes is and sometimes isn't after school. One block ahead, on Madison, seven police cars are lined up and a knot of officers surrounds a man whose hands are behind his head. I'm awash in scenarios, anticipating Ollie's questions about what he's done, what's happening, what they'll do to him. This kind of thing fascinates her and explaining it flummoxes me. How much should I tell her? What could this person have possibly done to require seven police cars and how could she ever understand it? As I'm thinking all this, she asks: Mama, did you see that squirrel up there scampering on the telephone line? She actually uses the word "scamper." By this point, we've passed the police cars, which she hasn't seen, and I have missed the scampering squirrel.

OCTOBER 13, 2013

We're riding home from school on one of the last warm afternoons of the year, Ollie on her bike, Viv on the back of the Xtracycle. I have remembered to bring a water bottle and it is filled with water! But it's hot and we are parched. When we stop to drink, we drain the bottle. We're only a mile from home, but the girls are clamoring for more water. Not just clamoring—whining. Ollie is almost crying. The row of tidy ranch houses near us have tended front lawns and Halloween decorations. "Who's not going to give us some of their water?" I think as I knock on the nearest door. No one answers. For some reason, I look up under the eaves above my head. There, drawn in peach chalk, is an enormous outline of a penis. Beneath it, the word LOVE. How this was drawn so high up there and why, I will never know. But it makes me smile and I'm glad for the surprise of it. We do find water, by the way, at the next house, from a nice man in sweats.

NOVEMBER 4, 2013

On our way to drop Vivie off at school, Ollie and I have a deal. Ollie can ride her bike alone through an unpaved alleyway to avoid taking two hills that I like to take. Ollie and I are to to meet on the other side, where she is supposed to stop at the edge of the gravel, ding her bell, and wait for me to ding my bell and wave her on. But, for some reason, the kid will not wait. Every time I get to the bottom of my hill, there she is, radiantly pedaling her bike toward me. I can see she is proud of herself—and I want her to feel confident and capable. But I'm also worried about cars not seeing her. "These people," I tell her, "they're putting on mascara and texting their girlfriends. They're not looking out for you." We talk about this, and it frustrates her to tears. I don't want to upset her before school, and so we move on, and then we do it again the next day. One day, there are actually two cars coming, one each way, and one of them going way too fast. I ding my bell, which is a ridiculous way to try to get the attention of someone in the capsule of her car, NPR blasting. Ollie hears my bell dinging and takes it as a signal to go. In response, I jump up and down and wave wildly at the cars. The cars pass; Ollie makes it to me, and I'm upset; she's confused. "But you rang the bell, Mama," she says.

November 13, 2013

Each day, Viv and I have exactly 40 minutes after I pick her up from school until we have to pick up Ollie. On this day, I have an errand to run—the simple mailing of a pre-paid package at the UPS store. But it's in the opposite direction of Ollie's school, and I'm worried about time. Anything can throw us off and make us late. If Viv has to poop or has an itch on her foot or if the street sweeper is in the bike path. But I am errand-hungry, like you get when you just want to cross this last thing off your list. And Viv is game. We take off, and the ride to the UPS store is both hillier and longer than I had remembered. This errand is an obstacle course—every stoplight, every car turning in front of us, every pothole. Viv is chanting, "Go, Mama, go." We wear our bike helmets into the store to save time. In line, we get behind two University of Oregon students mailing four pairs of Ugg boots to Japan. Each pair must be weighed separately. We are sweating in our helmets and jackets and making punchy chatter with the woman in line behind us. I finally make it to the front of the line while Viv turns and turns a rack of gift cards. The package mailed, we sail out the door and onto our bikes, up a hill, "Go Mama Go," and then the rhyming game: hark, bark, stark, park, lark, *matriarch!* And we make it to Ollie's school by 3:09 (pick up at 3:10).

DECEMBER 3, 2013

On the first frosty morning of the season, we bundle up, the girls stiff with layers of natural and un-natural fibered clothing—woolies plus regular clothes plus sweaters plus raingear plus two pairs of mittens, both wool and waterproof, then hats and helmets. Viv is wearing all the same clothes as she wore the day before, but, oh well, she's dressed, she's relatively clean and she's warm. We're feeling good getting out the door on time with no significant fits, which is striking

photo by Bob Passaro

when you consider the bunchiness of all those layers. Viv's on the back of the Xtracycle; Ollie's on her bike. A block away from home, rounding the first corner of our commute, Ollie's front tire slips on the frosty pavement, and she falls. It hits me in the gut, my kid in the middle of the road, splayed and crying. But she isn't hurt and no cars are coming. Viv stays balanced on the Xtracycle with its kickstand down, and I help Ollie to the parking strip where we inspect her knee through a fresh hole in her leggings. She's shaken but okay and says she wants to get back on the bike (moment of motherly pride!). That's when I notice a custard-y substance dripping down Viv's legs and into the panniers. What the hell? Then I remember the chickens' eggs we'd gathered at our neighbor's house the day before. What had we done with those four eggs? Yes, Viv had put them in her pockets. I scoop what's left of the yolk and whites and shells from her coat pockets and leave them on the curb. I make a mental note to go back and get them, but I never do.

MARCH 22, 2014

We are riding home from a birthday party, Ollie on her bike and Viv on the back of the Xtracycle, but with her two-wheeler (the smallest bike they make; it has twelve-inch wheels) in the panniers. We get to a hill and, for some reason, Viv insists on getting her bike out and riding up it. I know she can't ride up the hill—I can barely ride up it—but I'm worn down from the demands of the day and so I say okay, alright, let's give it a try. We stop, and she insists on unloading the bike from the panniers herself. Once the bike is out and she has painstakingly re-secured the buckles on the panniers, she tries to balance on the bike and start on the hill. She tries and tries and finally gives up and pushes her little bike up the hill. At the top of the hill, she wants to get back on and ride down a smaller hill. She gets back on the bike and starts riding down the hill, and she's doing great, really great, when I realize that the hill is steeper than I'd realized, that she's not ready for this hill. I'm riding behind her on the Xtracycle and Ollie is riding behind me on her bike. I'm thinking that I need to ditch the Xtracycle and grab Viv before she crashes, but she's going way too fast. I'm watching her, pedals now moving faster than her feet can keep up with. My powerlessness to prevent the certain crash is a parenting low point for me.

Viv crashes and goes over the handlebars. Ollie and I throw down our bikes and rush to her. A woman comes running from down the hill. Viv howls, her chin gushing blood. There is more blood than I've ever seen coming from a child of mine. The woman offers her cell phone and dials my husband's number because I'm too shaky. Bob doesn't answer. We are eight blocks from home, and we have more bike than will fit in the the woman's Volvo. We put Viv's bike back in the panniers and Viv on the back. She's whimpering now, and I am saying over and over, "You're fine, you're doing great, we're almost home." I am saying it for me as much as for her. At home, Bob inspects the wound and confirms that she will be fine, but a trip to the ER might be wise. At the hospital, she gets three stitches, during which they roll her in a blanket like a burrito to make sure that she doesn't thrash around, but she doesn't move, doesn't even cry. I shake for the rest of the day.

May 12, 2014

Viv breaks open the skin on her chin once again. Bob is with her this time—they are practicing braking on a hill in the church parking lot near our house. They come home; her chin is bloody, Bob is shaky, and and it is my turn to say she will be fine. Viv will be a member of the chin-scar-from-bike-accident(s)-club, as are at least half of the adults in our circles.

June 3, 2014

On our way to school, we are trying to cross a busy street. There is so much traffic, it is taking minutes longer than usual. "Ride a bike, people," I mutter uselessly. This cracks up the girls, and they start saying it, too. "Ride a bike, people!" Viv yells to each and every car. I am smiling, and I resist the urge to tell my sweet radical to tone it down. We finally get across and the driver of a large truck who has been waiting for us to cross so he can make a left turn barks at us that we should try crossing at the stoplight. "We probably should," I say reverting to the meek way I have with strangers who admonish me. And then, later, I realize, No, we shouldn't have to cross at the stoplight. The street with the stoplight is way busier than the one we're on. No, why doesn't he cross at the stoplight? Why hadn't I said that to Mr. Grumpy with his big fat carbon footprint?

A couple days later, Ollie makes posters that say "Ride a Bike!" They show happy, helmeted bike commuters and a bubble-shaped car with a slash through it. She knows about the slash from the signs people put in yards that show a slash through a pooping dog. We laminate Ollie's signs and staple them to telephone poles.

June 13, 2014

It's a Friday—Viv's day off of preschool—and we have extra time while we're running errands. We decide to finally buy her the new helmet she needs, a task I've been avoiding because I know it will not be easy (I might have mentioned she is stubborn, and she resists change). We visit Arriving by Bike, a commuter shop with friendly salespeople, and Viv latches onto a purple helmet with orange and pink flowers despite my best efforts at coaxing her into one that looks like an eight ball. She resists the helmet-fitting and buckle-tightening process, but the salesman is patient with her and explains the importance of a properly-fitting helmet. We leave the shop with her new $60 purple helmet snugly on her small head.

Later that day, we are riding to pick up Ollie at school, and Viv's fiddling with her new helmet, loosening it as much as she can. I tell her she needs to tighten it, and she doesn't want to, so she chucks the helmet onto the bike path. I stop. She gets off the Xtracycle and starts running down the bike path—in the right direction, at least. She will not ride, she says, if she has to wear the helmet. She will run. "Fine," I say, and ride after her on the bike. But she gets tired after a bit. It's now the time we're supposed to be picking up Ollie, and we're a mile away. I get off the bike and walk with her. I am trying to be patient, but I'm not succeeding. I hate to be late. Viv grabs a tree and butts her head into it, skinning her nose. She is crying now, and I hold her for a few minutes. "We have to keep moving," I say when she has calmed down. I try to get her back on the bike, but she won't. I begin walking again, now ten paces in front of her, saying—regrettably—kids who don't wear their helmets don't get to be kindergarteners next year. We arrive at Ollie's school 20 minutes late. We run to get Ollie and she's happily emptying recycling cans with her teacher. Everything in the elementary school world, it seems, is normal. Back at the bikes, Viv shows Ollie her new helmet. "Look," she says. "Isn't it cool?" She hops on the back of the Xtracycle and we are off.

Why We Ride

Amy Subach

Amy Subach, feminist, lives in Portland, Oregon with a neurotic dog, two children, and her husband. She enjoys thinking up creative comebacks to street harassment and looking at pictures of other people's children, but not in a creepy way. She feels very proud of herself when both of her kids have their nails clipped. Once, in high school, she spent a summer watching too much British television and talking in a terrible british accent. She's not afraid to lift heavy or to sing badly, as long as she has the appropriate drinks and attire. She would like to assure you that you are not going to ruin your child's brain. You can follow her on twitter @amysue or Instagram @amysuea.

If you think getting screaming kids into their car seats, then being trapped inside said car with them still screaming at you is frustrating, then maybe you should try family biking. Sure, the kids still scream in the bucket of your cargo bike or your trailer, but you can build community by sharing the screaming with all the passers-by.

Actually, kids scream a lot less on bikes, probably because riding a bike is a lot more fun than being in a car, even in the rain. Most of the time.

Portland may be slipping in the ranks as America's top city for people on bikes, but it has a growing contingent of families who bike to school and the grocery store and the park. A lot of parents here are realizing that they can sell one of their cars, invest in a cargo bike or a bike trailer or one of the other many kid carrying configurations, and make their daily slogs a little more fun for everybody. And peer pressure is totally at work. As more parents take up biking with kids, other parents who used to think that there's no way they could do it have started to reconsider their options, even if it's just because they feel embarrassed being the only one doing the school drop-off in an SUV.

I'm a member of the PDX Cargo Bike Gang on Facebook. We mostly talk about the hows and whys of riding with kids and plan donut meet-ups. I asked the members to tell me why they started riding with their kids. Here are some of the best answers, quoted with permission.

Some parents replied that they were simply carrying on their past habits. Bike mom Joyanna Eisenberg wrote, "I fell in love with biking on my own first, and then I wanted the kids to be a part of it."

Other parents said that they see bicycling as a necessity. Bike dad Matt Hannafin wrote: "Since I work from home, we've never been able to justify having more than one car, which my wife drives to work. However, when it came time for our son to start preschool, it was also logical for me (since I make my own schedule) to be the one to do drop-off and pick-up. We definitely didn't want a second car, since that just seemed unethical. The logical solution, then, was a bike. I considered a trailer, but then decided on a cargo bike because it seemed to offer more connection with the kids while riding—which it does."

Sometimes, it takes a kick in the pants from the universe to get you on a bike. Janine Eckhart's car was stolen when her daughter was 10 months old. Switching to bikes was something she "was ethically drawn to, but hadn't given a ton of practical thought to." More than four years and one more daughter later, she's still riding and "super grateful to that car thief."

There are lots of great reasons to bike with your kids: it saves money, it's good exercise, it sets a good example, and "it makes my kids tough, smart and balanced," as Roberta Robles wrote. But above all else, biking with your kids is super fun.

Every time I'm out with my cargo bike, picking my daughter up from preschool or getting groceries with my infant son, a young kid will pull her mom's hand over towards my bike to ogle at it, or a grandpa will pace around my bike at the park, or, as happened when I was 39 weeks pregnant and at the grocery store loading up my haul and my four-year-old, a mom will walk over just to congratulate me.

My bike causes a scene and it sparks a light in people's eyes. I can almost see the gears turning: If that waddling pregnant lady with the crying preschooler can get groceries on her bike, then anyone can.

Biking with kids isn't always easy. But it's easy for a lot of us to forget that driving is even harder, and in ways that aren't nearly as satisfying as getting that screaming kid, your groceries, and your cursing self up that hill in the rain.

wheelwomen.switchboardhq.com

∽❧ **REVIEWS** ❧∽

RIDE
Short Fiction About Bicycles

Stories by

S.J. Rozan

Kent Peterson

Barb Goffman

Paul Guyot

Keith Snyder

Simon Wood

Barbara Jaye Wilson

and others

ebooks & print • twitter.com/ridebikefiction

Women & Cycling Zines:
Something for Just About Everyone

Julie Brooks

Bicycling zines first appeared as homespun collections of prose, poetry, pictures, and drawings compiled in slim, compact, often-peculiar little notebooks that fit in a purse, small bag, or even in one's back pocket. The mostly-handwritten stories and sometimes-blurry photos were generally Xeroxed, black and white (some with colored cover pages), stapled, and distributed—either for free or for a minimal amount of money by their DIY producers. They were awesome in their simplicity and candor. In the past 20 years these modest pedaling jotters have certainly evolved. Some have shiny, crisp covers with dedicated margins around personal narratives and critical essays, while others showcase sharp photographic images and multi-colored sketches. And, still, some remain modest and raw.

I enjoyed the opportunity to peruse four (and a half) of the newest women-authored, -edited, and -illustrated zines to come out in the burgeoning women and bicycling community. And, wow, did I enjoy the ride!

WE RIDE BICYCLES: A BIKE ZINE BY WOMEN FOR EVERYBODY

A project by Annie Dunkel & Shell Stern,

Charlotteville, VA

$5 from takingthelane.com

This black-and-white compendium includes lyrical and reflective essays, pictures, and design instructions for a DIY bike hat and a spoke card. It certainly doesn't disappoint. Geared toward the female bicycle rider who doesn't race or wear only Spandex, Dunkel and Stern have culled a collection of essays that provide glimpses into the lives of those who commute and ramble by bike. Specifically, they've provided space for the voices of moms who bicycle with their kids in tow, an environmental policy professor who espouses an appreciation for the ecology of transport, and a woman obsessed with being seen by drivers, creating and donning reflective, flashy, and fun clothing for the pedaler who doesn't want to have to carry an extra set of clothing to work. There are also essays about bike polo, living and riding in other countries, the power of friendship while pumping up long, steep hills, pedicabbing, and the simple beauty of the "big, dorky, comfy, fat-ass bike seat."

I found these essays to be wonderfully confirming of the inherent utilitarian and liberatory possibilities of the bicycle for women. Riders do not have to wear "hi-viz" clothing to be seen. Moms don't have to be super-powered to pedal their children up hills. And chainsaws don't need to be transported in the back of a Ford F150 truck.

Velo Vixen, #2: A Zine About Women and Bicycling

Edited by Rachel Krause, Kansas City, MO

$4 from velovixenzine.com

or

takingthelane.com

Like its predecessor, volume #2 of Velo Vixen is a rough, spirited celebration of women who ride bikes. There are tributes to parents who inspired, encouraged, and fretted about young ones growing up and exploring the world on two wheels; wonderfully evocative snapshots of bikes, women, and women on bikes; poetry lauding the untrammeled freedom one experiences while pedaling past anxiety-ridden motorists; inspiring quotes; amusing how-to lessons on transforming your bike trailer into a mobile café; and getting the most out of Missouri's own "Pedaler's Jamboree." I was especially moved by Roam Oliver's timely essay on training for her ride across Kansas. In words both raw and redolent of a certain kind of hell, Oliver made me feel like I was pedaling alongside her, scurrying up and plunging down both the trails and emotional rollercoasters she was exploring in the weeks leading up to her trip across the sunflower state. In the introduction to this volume, Rachel Krause writes that the stories within are "emotional, brutally honest, yet empowering." By the time I closed this pint-size digest of turbulent and inspiring tales, I was ready for a luxurious nap.

ZOOM!

By Jennifer Charrette & Marcia Kinne,

Illustrated by Kellie Day, Ridgeway, CO

$9.95 from takingthelane.com

It's hard to call *Zoom!* a zine. And, perhaps, I should stay with the publisher's (our own, Elly Blue's) description of "adventure book." Still, it's small and thin, larger than a back pocket might accommodate, but certainly purse- or iPad-bag sized. It's a wonderfully colorful and inviting little booklet; a story about the adventures of a tyke on his run-bike. Axel scurries his Strider balance bike through the world with an abandon few of us remember, but all of us should strive to recapture. He was a small courier with a huge message: "Wheeeeeeeeeee!"

Though this tiny package is chock-full of amazing energy, I felt compelled to look a little deeper into Axel's story after noting that in the introduction to the book, Professional Road Cyclist, George Hincapie, hopes that readers will enjoy reading *Zoom!*, and that they will "share it with the same passion that Axel had for life." "Had for life?" I asked myself when I finished. What did that mean? I'll leave it to you to investigate further the story of Axel's death. It's certainly not a need-to-know element of *Zoom!*, though it might contextualize things a bit regarding the larger Axel Project, which benefits from the sale of each book.

Suffice it to say that Axel's energy, like that of many little ones who are encouraged and supported to live their lives with vim and vigor from the get-go, is infectious. I have two nephews who are now well beyond the years of traveling around by balance bike, but whose zest for life atop two wheels was easily recalled when I picked up and devoured *Zoom!*

This book really is a gem. And it doesn't hurt that there's a pup—a golden retriever, perhaps—running alongside the two-wheeled adventurer on just about every page.

SADDLE, SORE: A WOMEN-ONLY GUIDE TO YOU AND YOUR BIKE

By Molly Hurford

$16 from saddlesorewomen.com

or

takingthelane.com

Molly Hurford's zine is more like a shiny, smallish book. Its simple cover depicts a woman on her bike, standing while pedaling a flat stretch of road through town, which brings one to immediately assume that—given the title of this little tome—she's trying to avoid the nasty burn of saddle sores. Hurford's book is a funny, fascinating, and disturbing examination of a woman's anatomy down there, both on and off of the bike. Above all it is demystifying, taking on a topic most people cringe to think about and gasp at in horror when mentioned aloud. Covering everything from the basic composition of saddles and chamois to that "extra large pimple" that hurts like the dickens, menstruation, sex, and how to talk to your coach and bike shop staff about pain and what you need, *Saddle, Sore* is a must read for women who ride bikes.

I found Chapter Five, "Saddle Sores," offers some of the most illuminating information for me, if only because Hurford makes clear, with the assistance of cycling coaches and doctors, that not every "little bump down there" is a full-fledged saddle sore. Silly as it may seem, though a pedaler for most of my life, it's only been in the past couple of years that I've had to contend with sore spots on my rump. Who knew there were variations? And not all of those blistery little pimples were just waiting to emerge as red, hot, swollen mounds of puss? Okay, if the verbiage in that last question made you feel a little queasy, be forewarned that Hurford's book is full of such expressions. But please don't let this discourage you, for the information Hurford conveys is both poignant and invaluable. This is a book that everyone in the bicycling community needs to read and share.

I Am a Beast on Two Wheels

By BikePGH's Women and Biking Program

Find this zine when it comes out at

bikepgh.org/womenbike

Hallelujah for the opportunity to take a sneak peak of the forthcoming women and bikes zine out of Pittsburgh, PA. In deference to their first volume, the organizers of the Women and Biking Program invited local women (and men) who bike, don't bike, are considering biking, or simply support any of these choices to hang out, share stories and co-create what looks like another vibrant assemblage of poetic and imaginative revelry for the bicycle in women's lives. Since the final zine hasn't yet come out, I'll simply offer a few teasers, dear reader, and suggest that you won't fully appreciate the beauty of your lobster claws this winter— and perhaps haven't yet celebrated the perks of having a fro—until you've flipped through the amusing pages of this spunky compilation.

⇐

Editor's note: It's in the nature of zines to go out of print. We'll do our best to make the ones reviewed here available or let you know how to find them until we can't track down any more copies. If the one you want has fallen off the radar, please take it as a challenge and an inspiration to make your own.

∽ **PARTING SHOT** ∾

Definition

Lindsay Kandra

Lindsay Kandra is an intermittent bike racer, professional problem-solver, and amateur social satirist. She lives in Portland, Oregon with three spastic dogs, two fed-up cats, and a human being that is really good at keeping the kitchen clean.

fem·i·nism /ˈfe-mə-ˌni-zəm/. Noun. The belief that all genders and all bodies should be treated with dignity and respect, and that all genders and bodies should have equitable access to safety, education, wealth, health care, and custom-built steel gravel touring frames with disc brakes.

See Also: Equal Pay (and race payouts), Title IX, Universal Health Care, Birth Control, Paternity Leave, Ruth Bader Ginsberg, Margaret Atwood, Elizabeth Warren, Marianne Vos, Beyoncé, Marriage for Anyone Crazy Enough to Take the Plunge, Feeling Guilty About Using PMS to Get Out of Submitting Timesheets on Time.

Antonyms: the glass ceiling, fat-shaming, slut-shaming, mommy-shaming, gay-bashing, DOMA, photoshop, rape, genital mutilation, censorship, racism, ableism, illiteracy, toxic masculinity, religious fundamentalism, Bill O'Reilly, Clarence Thomas.

What does feminism mean to you?

SUBSCRIBE TO EVERYTHING WE PUBLISH!

Do you love what Microcosm publishes?

Do you want us to publish more great stuff?

Would you like to receive each new title as it's published?

Subscribe as a BFF to our new titles and we'll mail them all to you as they are released!

$10-30/mo, pay what you can afford. Include your t-shirt size and month/date of birthday for a possible surprise! Subscription begins the month after it is purchased.

microcosmpublishing.com/bff

...AND HELP US GROW YOUR SMALL WORLD!